It's My Life

by Charles C. Palmer

iUniverse, Inc.
Bloomington

It's My Life

iUniverse books may be ordered through booksellers or by contacting:

iUniverse
1663 Liberty Drive
Bloomington, IN 47403
www.iuniverse.com
1-800-Authors (1-800-288-4677)

ISBN: 978-1-4697-3247-3 (sc)
ISBN: 978-1-4697-3249-7 (hc)
ISBN: 978-1-4697-3248-0 (e)

Printed in the United States of America

iUniverse rev. date: 05/14/2012

Contents

Acknowledgments

I am fortunate to have a wonderful family and friends who were generous with their time, thinking, and listening skills, thus encouraging me to finish this project. Your support and encouragement are not unnoticed.

I thank my family members for their confidence in me and all the help and support they gave. Special thanks to Vanessa, who did all of the typing for me. I know it wasn't an easy task sitting at the computer for hours. To my dearest wife, Zenneth, thanks for your patience and support and for listening to all my stories.

I also want to say a special thank-you to Dr. Euan Menzies for his encouragement to my family and me throughout the years and for being a family doctor to us. May God continue to bless you! Thank you!

Finally, I glorify God for His kindness and blessings on my life.

Introduction

Have you ever dreamed of flying free from all life's hardships and complications? Being free to do what you want, how you want, when you want? Well, that's how I felt most of my childhood life. I was just dying to break free from the constant rules, tough chores, and chaos. I just wanted to fly free and be whoever I wanted to be.

This book recaps my life experiences by showing some good and bad times but speaks mostly about the hardships I endured. I wanted to introduce my children, grandchildren, and great-grandchildren to the adversities I had to undergo while growing up, which made me the man I am today. I also wanted to educate the general reading public that life wasn't always as easy as it is today with things being so freely obtained; so many choices of food, clothing, and education; or so many privileges being given to children.

I hope that, after reading this book, one would appreciate the life he has more and stop taking things for granted. One would really be thankful for the blessings that have been bestowed upon him, and he would be indebted to his parents or persons who raised him to be who he is today.

Chapter One

Childhood Days: Fun and Hard

I am a product of the island of Providenciales in the Turks and Caicos, particularly the settlement of Wheeland, where I was born and bred. I'm a child of the 1950s, so the great change in child rearing and comforts of life in such a short time totally amaze me. It is very clear to me since I still live in Wheeland.

My parents, grandparents, and stepparents were all from Turks and Caicos, and almost all of them were from Wheeland. My stepmother was originally from Lorimers, Middle Caicos, another island in the Turks and Caicos, and so was my stepfather. As a teenager, my mother spent some time with relatives in Lorimers, where she met and married my stepfather.

My mother's and stepfather's marriage didn't last very long because her husband went away shortly after the wedding and didn't return for many years. With the approval of her mother-in-law, who felt that her son had mistreated and disrespected his wife and didn't deserve her, she began to date again. She met and took interest in my father, Thomas Palmer. Now during this courtship, Thomas was married to the lovely Altiny Penn. But he convinced this shy and timid young Emily that this relationship could work. Vulnerable and lonely, she fell for it. You see, Thomas wasn't handsome, but he was cool and knew how to woo the ladies.

Thomas, the son of Joseph and Jane Palmer of Blue Hills, Providenciales, grew up in Blue Hills and attended school there until he was old enough to go fishing. He would go in the dinghy boat with his father to row the boat for him—that is, to be the sculler—while he got fish, conch, or lobster. The men at that time always wished for a son or two when their wife was expecting a baby, so they could go in the boat with them as soon as they turned twelve or thirteen years old. Unfortunately, they weren't concerned about giving these boys an education. The challenge was to see which boat could bring in the most fish, conch, or lobster for the week or duration of time they were out. Sometimes, they stayed out for two weeks. Daughters were expected to stay home and learn to keep house or look after younger children. They also helped out in the fields and gardens.

My father wasn't a good fisherman, but he was a good boatman and knew how to save money. So as a young man, he saved the money he earned from fishing. Sometimes the men got to go on freight liners to different countries of the world. These trips lasted longer than the fishing trips and were completely different. When my father thought he had saved enough money, he began building a house. It wasn't easy to obtain cement in those days, so he resorted to building a lime kiln. This lime kiln was as tall as he was and about twenty feet in circumference. He used this white lime, along with a few bags of cement when it was available from Grand Turk, our country's capital, or East Harbor, now known as South Caicos, to build the first phase of his house. Upon completion, he lived in it alone since he was still unmarried.

In those days, only one fishing plant was in Turks and Caicos, so fishermen from around the islands had to go to South Caicos to carry their catch to the Caicos fisheries. On one of his trips there, my father met a young girl, Altiny Penn, the daughter of Mr. and Mrs. Daniel Penn of Middle Caicos. At that time, she was living in East Harbor with her older sister Hennessy Jennings. These two young people fell in love and soon realized they couldn't live without each other. So one year and six months later, they were married.

My father was always a hard worker and wanted the best for his family. At this point, he began to make plans to build his own boat. Mr. Algernon Dean, one of the best boat builders then, built his first boat for him. Thomas was so proud of this achievement that he named it after his young wife, the *Altiny*.

Their marriage only produced one child, a daughter who lived less than a year, Heartlyn. They didn't have any more children as a couple. My father had many children with other women, my mother being one of them. She stuck with him and had six children for him. I was her firstborn, and then came Stanley, Yvonne, Jacinth, Mackey, and Lynn. Two other women had three more children with him as well.

Our stepmother, Altiny, cared for most of us as if we were her own. She took my sister Francis and me to live with her. She loved me and treated me special. Since she didn't have any children of her own, she asked my mother to give me to her when I was nine months old.

Now, my mother was a married woman who was beautiful, young, and ambitious. Many men admired her, but she chose to stay with my father. Many of the women around became intimidated by her and began to accuse her of being with their husbands and male friends. So they suggested many possible fathers for me. Because of my complexion and hair texture at birth, they even thought a white man had fathered me. I don't know how they came up with that idea, but I'm happy that my father accepted me and was very proud of me. In those days, white people were seldom seen here. Natives wouldn't have gotten that close to them. They were taught to hold whites in high regard, so much so that they would even treat them better than themselves. I believed my mother when she told me my father was Thomas Palmer. If she waited five years for her husband, what made them think she didn't know who fathered her child! As I grew up and caught wind of all these different stories, I assumed or envisioned my life would be hard, and so it was.

My stepmother used to show me off; especially to those who didn't know that she didn't have any children or had forgotten. Ma Tiny, as I called her, was a strong swimmer. She taught me to swim when I was about two years old. As a boy, I spent a lot of time at the beach. Back then, we would say, "We are going on the bay."

At times, the fishing boats were brought in to be cleaned, painted, or repaired. The crewmembers would go to the beach early and wait for the high tide before they pulled their boats in. While they waited, they told each other stories they had heard or stories about their families. I liked to sit and listen to them talk about the olden days, tales of fishing, and other adventures they'd had.

The crewmembers were usually the men who had dinghy boats. The sloops, sailing boats, towed these. Sometimes, one sloop pulled a number of dinghy boats. The dingy owner paid a towage fee to the sloop owner at the end of the fishing week. The boats usually came back into port on Saturday mornings. I can still remember the white sails flopping in the wind, each pulling five or six dinghys in its wake. These trips back home always turned into a race. The fishermen families assembled on the beach and watched to see which boat would win and who would come in second. This was a regular fun activity for the entire community. It was like watching a well-organized regatta.

Most of the women and men who didn't fish worked the fields and raised corn, peas, potatoes, sugarcane, and other produce. Still, they took time out to go to the beach, watch the race, and hear the men announce who got the most lobster or conch. Some women stayed home and made clothes for the people of the community and baked breads and cakes for sale. On Saturdays, nearly everyone washed, ironed, baked bread, fried fish, and made everything ready for Sunday because, on Sunday mornings, nothing was better than some stewed fish and potato bread before attending church.

Men who didn't go fishing on the sloops for the week would go out to the reef or in the harbor and catch fish and conch to sell along the shore. Back then, people lived neighborly. They were kind and gave to the needy and less fortunate. Even if you didn't have money, you would still go home with fish or conch because the fishermen gave to the people whatever they needed. Back then, the fellowship between neighbors was really close-knit. The strangers among us weren't left out. They, too, were treated with kindness.

The older folks always told the younger ones, "Treat people kindly because you don't know where you or your children will have to go."

To declare the winning sloop, conch shell horns were blown in a certain order from the crowd. After the boats had been anchored, cleaned, and tidied, the men would go home and spend time with their families. In the evening, they would meet at Mr. Paul Grant's house, the town meeting house. There were no bars or nightclubs established then. Mr. Grant, a natural-born comedian, made everyone laugh. He could make you laugh if you were crying or make you laugh until you cried. That's a fact.

The men would get together and make excuses for the boats that lost the race, complain about the others who caused the boat to lose by not doing the right thing or making the right decision, and brag about the boat that won. While they fussed, they drank gallons and gallons of monkey bag, a Haitian rum made from the sugarcane known as *claran* (similar to moonshine). They sat around for hours and talked about boat races, lobster, conch, turtles, scale fish, sponge, girls, and sometimes money. Later in the evening, when they began to feel the effects from the cane liquor, some got into fights as a result of the continuous arguments. Some fell asleep anywhere they could lay their heads to sleep off the liquor effect and immediately start drinking again once they awoke.

I used to feel sorry for my father when he got drunk. He wasn't much of a drinker, and when he drank, he would be sick for two days.

I always knew when he had been drinking. He would begin to sing as soon as he got to the door of his house. I do not know if he knew any secular songs, but he always sang the chorus, "Somewhere beyond the blue, there's a mansion for you." (This is a Christian chorus.) He always used to ask me to hold his hand, walk to the bedroom with him, and stay to keep his company. I liked it sometimes.

He was never really a fighter either. He preferred to be known as a lover. However, he pushed a left jab on someone once, knocking the man out cold. He was at his weakest at the sight of a rat. For a long time, I didn't know what we were running from. He just started running, so I did too. One night while we were singing, he looked up and suddenly jumped to his feet and ran. I was right behind; looking around to try to figure out what frightened him so much. Eventually, I saw a fat rat in the corner, almost the size of a kitten. I was sure that thing had to be dangerous for my father to be so afraid, and so, to this day, I am the same way. I don't ever go near a rat, dead or alive. Sometimes Ma Tiny would be in the kitchen baking bread, cleaning her peas, or taking corn off the cob to dry. We would run to her, and she would know what had happened. Houses back then weren't sealed like we make them today. Storage areas were open, where produce was laid out to dry or ripen. This encouraged rats. Corn, peas, potatoes, cassava, and even salt fish and dried conch had to be brought inside in the evening for protection from animals.

We didn't know about kerosene, gas, or electric stoves in those days. We cooked outside the house on firewood. Baking was done with coal made from wood. Some ovens were made out of sixty-gallon drums with the door cut in the side; others were made of bricks. The men made the grid out of steel and mounted it above the coal stove so the heat could be distributed evenly. Most ovens had two layers or grids and could hold four pans of two loaves of bread each. These homemade ovens baked the most beautiful-looking bread. Ma Tiny was the best at baking nice, brown, soft, sweet-tasting bread. I still believe she was one of the best cooks in Turks and Caicos.

The fire hearth was made in basically the same way. The grid was longer, and instead of being enclosed as like the ovens, it was open. There was enough space in this rectangular table-like form to hold two or three cooking pots at the same time. Dried stalks were broken into nearly even pieces, bundled, and carried home on our heads. If wood ran out before the weekend, I had to get up early in the morning before I went to school to find more. I didn't like it. On Saturday mornings, however, most people were gathering wood, so I had company.

There weren't any tanks or cisterns to hold water, so we collected it in sixty-gallon drums. As I got older, it was my job to keep them full. We had about four of them, two for fresh rainwater to drink and two for water drawn from the wells for cooking, doing the laundry, and cleaning. Three wells were nearby: Forbes, Nelly, and Cow. The freshest one was Forbes. Cow had the most water beetle, and Nelly was the deepest. Sometimes, we had to get up in the night and go out to get water from the wells if there was a drought.

Only the basics were available. We didn't have electricity or all the conveniences we take for granted today. We used kerosene lamps then. But when oil was scarce, we only used it during emergencies. In the evenings, around a big fire outside, the family gathered to roast corn and potatoes. The fire provided light. Old ghost stories and stories about Brer Booky and Brer Yabbie were told. Brer Yabbie was the smart one, and Brer Booky could never figure out that he was being made a fool of.

My chores were many as a growing boy. Ma Tiny awakened me at five o'clock nearly every morning. Oftentimes, I didn't get up right away when she called me. I wouldn't know a thing until I felt cold water in my face and all over the rest of my body and bed. I had to get up and start my chores in those wet clothes. I first had to fill one of the drums with water from the wells. This had to be done by six thirty. Then I had to go into the bushes to gather a bundle of wood. On my return, I cleaned around the yard. To top it off, I would crack about eight quarts of corn before I went to school.

Our toilets were latrines or outhouses. Keeping the latrine clean was another part of my responsibility. I had to sweep it out every day and scrub it once a week, as well as throw the ash left from the burned wood into the toilet hole to keep the scent down.

I hardly ever got to school on time, and the teacher often flogged me for being late. I was kept working in the mornings, and as school time drew near, Ma Tiny would stand in the southern door of the house where she could see the school's flag high up on its pole. Only when she saw the flag descending would she allow me to get ready for school. Although I was already late, I had to eat my breakfast and bathe before I left for school. You could image how fast I had to prepare myself, knowing I would be the laughing stock of the school when I got called for my flogging. The teachers used raw cowhide or leather for a whip. I would have to change hands to ease the pain.

My lateness was so common that the children used to talk about it at recess whether I was present or not. They didn't seem to respect me. They joked about the amount of work I had to do before coming to school. The really arrogant ones even bragged how they could sleep until eight o'clock and then just come to school. Their parents did everything for them. I decided I was going to put a stop to their bragging and earn their respect another way. Guess how? I learned to fight!

The embarrassment made me angry, and I wanted the disrespect to go away. So I began to slap or punch those haughty children who made fun of me. The teacher didn't appreciate me fighting the students so I would get more flogging for that. I never was flogged about my lessons because I made sure I knew that. I wanted to learn as much as I could and always did my best at my schoolwork.

At home, my stepmother often flogged me for fighting because my combatants or their parents would tell her about it. Then she would let me have it. She would sometimes teach me at the kitchen table if there wasn't any more work to do. She wasn't as bright as I thought she was. I knew I was spelling a word correctly, but she would say it was wrong and spank me for it. When I found out she didn't know as much as I thought she did, I cried because she often told my father I was dumb. I knew he might take me out of school and carry me into the boat to scull for him. My father was a better scholar than she was, but he never made any effort to test my knowledge. I guess he believed her when she concluded I wasn't learning anything.

Sometimes I was allowed to spend a week at a time with my mother in Corinize. I enjoyed those visits because I got to spend more time playing with my cousins and not just doing chores. My mother didn't have as many material things as my stepmother did, but I didn't mind it much. For example, when I went to school while I was at her house, she would give me boiled sweet potato or cassava with boiled conch. This would be placed in a half-gallon paint kettle that was cleaned properly by using saltwater and sand. It was covered tightly. By lunchtime, everything in the kettle would be purple. Sometimes the bigger boys would take it from me and show it around to the others who could afford to bring something they thought was better. The sweet potato was cooked with the skin attached and placed into the kettle while still hot. So steam building up in the sealed kettle released natural purple dye, contained in the sweet potato skin, which would discolor the rest of the food. I didn't mind eating lunch that my mother gave me when I was at her home. Sometimes I would carry bread if she baked during the weekdays. Overall, she fed me well. I was never hungry at her house. There was one negative feeling at Mummy's though. It seemed darker at night than it did at Daddy and Ma Tiny's house.

At home when I lay down to sleep, I would be in bed, which was made up on the floor, listening to the crickets and watching jack-o-lanterns through the seams in the wood. I would imagine all sorts of things. And most of all, she had a picture of her dead friend, Mae Forbes, lying in her casket, on the wall. This lady was one of the teachers in Riding Point, The Gap when I went to Grand Bahama, Bahamas. It made me afraid and unable to sleep. Sometimes I slept with my cousin, which made me feel better.

School could be fun sometimes, especially after I taught the bullies respect. On Wednesdays, the teachers had the responsibility of giving each child in school a cup of milk to aid in nutrition. Many families were unable to provide this essential nutrient for their children. The Education Department sent powdered milk to the school that the teachers would scald before serving. For this purpose, they used large containers that originally contained lard or shortening. The boys were responsible for fetching firewood to heat the milk mixture. It was fun fetching wood because we were doing it with friends and it didn't seem like work. Each child had to bring a cup to receive his milk in. After everyone had a turn, we could go for seconds. Sometimes we would have thirds and end up sick. But that didn't stop us from doing the same thing the next week.

I realized I wasn't able to keep up with most of my peers who were attending school weekly, but I tried very hard when I was present to learn all I could. For most of my childhood, I spent one week attending school and the other week doing whatever work the adults were involved in at the time: fishing, going in the field, weeding the shrubs out of the crops, or working with sisal. For a child, all of those activities were hard work, but I had to do it. Other children had to help their parents with household chores, but not to the extent I had to or at the expense of missing whatever education was available at that time.

Eventually, at the tender age of thirteen, my father took Ma Tiny's advice and pulled me out of school for good. Right then, I became an official fisherman earning a living among the grown men. At times, we worked the sisal and took it to South Caicos for sale. Other times, we made ropes for the boat. Working with the sisal was very hard work and time consuming. The green plants had to be cut, stripped, bundled, and buried in the sand for a specific amount of time. Then it had to be dug up, bruised, washed in the saltwater, rinsed with fresh water, and then laid out to dry. After drying, it was cleared and placed in bundles to sell or be used for making rope, slippers, purses, or bags.

After the sisal had soaked in the water for a time, it developed a foul odor. The one doing the bruising would have that same odor on him after working in it all day. Particles of the soaked brown substance would be all over one's entire body at the end of the day. Late in the evening when I was finished working the sisal, I referred to myself as looking like a ghost and smelling like a horse. I embraced this opportunity to take a good swim and get most of the stuff washed off before going home to have a bath. I always used as little water as possible since I was the one responsible for keeping the family adequately supplied with water.

After working sisal close to Christmastime, we would take it into East Harbor (now South Caicos) to sell. We didn't get much money but took what we could get to ensure that we were prepared for Christmas. Before I became a full-fledged fisherman, I only visited South Caicos about twice a year, so I became very excited when I found out we were going there. Those were my best days as a young boy growing up. It took a whole day and a half to beat down the Caicos Banks with a southeast breeze blowing. I would be so filled with excitement, not allowing myself to fall asleep while we waited for the tide to rise so it would lift the boat over the sandbar at Milton Cay.

A tower with multicolored lights shone beautifully on heaps of salt in the distance. I felt that it was like going to heaven. In Blue Hills where we lived, there were no lights or lighthouses yet, and so to a boy, this was the life. If we got into South Caicos at night, everyone would go to sleep until the morning, but not me. I would sit all night in the cabin door, watch the lighthouse on Dove Cay, and listen to the sounds of generators running.

The first time I saw a moving truck, I was terrified of it. I thought it was an animal. I couldn't imagine what the headlights or the taillights were, and I was too scared to go near them at first. Life in East Harbor was very different from what I was used to in Blue Hills.

I especially liked it when we went shopping after having sold our sisal, dried conch, or fish. We would treat ourselves with a delicious native meal of peas and rice and fried bonefish. Man, if it were Christmastime, we would be going from shop to shop looking, for instance, for cloth to make new dresses for Ma Tiny. Seldom would we buy anything for my father or me.

One Christmas, what I wanted more than anything was one of those pistols that shot paper bullets. (Folks my age can remember those.) I did get it one Christmas and, with it, a cowboy hat and a harmonica too. I was set, contented, and satisfied. As I am reminded of those pleasurable trips to East Harbor, the fun I had playing with my pistols, wearing my cowboy hat, and making music with my harmonica, I realize there was, after all, an element of enjoyment during my formative years. I was the "singing cowboy."

I spent a short time in Grand Bahama at about the age of seven. Many persons of our country migrated to the Bahamas at that time to improve their standard of living. My father and stepmother did the same, and took me with them. We did not stay very long. That was fun too. I went to school along with my step-cousins. The late Reverend Peter Hall of Mount Olivet Baptist Church in South Caicos and Sydrian Pratt were teachers there. They always knew how to heat up my backside when I got involved in a fight, which happened often. My friends and I enjoyed making box carts with one wheel and two handles. These were similar to a wheelbarrow. On Friday afternoons and Saturdays, we would go to the bus stop and watch people come and go while we played.

One time when we were preparing to go to Grand Bahama, my father decided he wanted to go for a change since nearly everyone was going to work the pine yard. He wanted to stay only a short time though. We still had the *Altiny* then. To leave Turks and Caicos, it was necessary to go via Grand Turk with the full crew and passengers to clear immigration. Often on these trips, the passengers would get sick because crossing the ocean between South Caicos and Grand Turk could get rough.

After obtaining the necessary clearance, the boat would stop back in Blue Hills to take on water and give the women passengers a few hours to wash their clothes and revive from seasickness before sailing for the Bahamas. This was necessary because it took nearly a week to sail down to Grand Turk and back to Blue Hills in the sloop even though the voyage was only about seventy-seven miles. The extra time spent in Blue Hills never posed a problem with the government officials because communication was almost nonexistent. There was no way to inform authorities the boat had stopped in Blue Hills for a short time. Everyone would anxiously await our return from the Bahamas to see what relatives and close friends had sent to them. Some people would get clothes, wholesale groceries, or money.

Mayaguana is the first Bahamas Island en route from Blue Hills to Nassau, so all the boats going to and coming from the Bahamas stopped there. These trips usually took about three or four days. Customs & Immigration were available in Nassau for entrance into the Bahamas. After getting the necessary things done, some passengers would disembark at Nassau. Fresh groceries and water would be taken on before the boat set sail for Grand Bahama.

Back to the trip my father came on ... We sailed to Riding Point, The Gap, in Pine Ridge. I fell in love with it. There was plenty of pinewood to cut. My father and the other men wanted a better life for their families, and we stayed there for two years. The boat wasn't in use during this period, and we had to secure her as best we could.

We put her in a creek under some big trees to shade her from the sun. When the men went out to work an extended time, the boys took care of the boat. My cousins and I would go to the creek before school, check the boat, and wet the deck to help keep her from getting damaged by the sun. We stayed with my stepmother's sister, Mrs. Amanda Outten. I think Ma Tiny had the biggest family ever.

It didn't take me long to learn my way around the town. I enjoyed the smell of those old trucks and cars. Mr. Cash and Mr. Pinder were two of the community leaders, some of the white Bahamians. They were called "conkey joe." They had lovely orchards with different fruits. We had to pass their yard to go to the boat, admiring the bananas and guavas and sometimes picking grapes from the vine.

The streets were named for the letters of the alphabet and in order. The conkey joes, or white people, lived in A Town. B Town was where the stores and community church were located. They used this same church for school. We lived in D Town. The Church of God of Prophecy was in F Town. Mr. Bub Ferguson owned the bar just down the road from the church. He had a rum called "Green Seal." I first heard about it when my father and his friends talked about drinking it at the bar.

The streets were laid east to west. If you wanted to get from north to south, you had to take a footpath through someone's yard or walk to the nearest end of the street. There was only one bus stop then where we could catch a ride to the dock.

The supermarket was a boat named the *Robert Fulton* (after the inventor of the first commercially successful steamboat in America in 1807). Now the payroll office was also on the *Robert Fulton*, so on Fridays, the men would go to the dock to get paid. The wives would meet them there so they could purchase groceries and other necessities for the next week.

On these pay days, my friends and I obtained a free ride on the bus or house car with our box carts. When we got to the dock, we stood at the exit and waited for the women coming out with their groceries. We asked if they needed help because the bus was parked about two hundred feet from the *Robert Fulton*. Some would reward us with sixpence or one shilling. (The currency at that time was pounds, shillings, and pence.) At the end of the day, we often made as much as five shillings.

We had another well-paying job. On Sunday mornings before going to church, we shined shoes, a very good business because everyone going to church enjoyed looking good. For recreation, we went fishing off the bridge. We had it made because, on one side of the bridge, we could catch saltwater fish and, on the other side, freshwater fish. After catching saltwater fish, we simply shifted sides to catch freshwater fish.

The soil in the area where we lived was very fertile. Fruits and vegetables grew everywhere in large quantities. There were pigeon peas, cassava, tomatoes, cane, and avocado, almost anything you could think of. Food grew wild. We never went hungry. We could always find something to eat without having to cook a meal.

One day, we were taking a trip from Riding Point, The Gap, to Marco City, and on to Sea Grape. Ma Tiny was going to visit one of her sisters, Mrs. Fairlaine Lightbourne. We were riding with her nephew Junior Outten (The Big Mock). The drive was long, and we stopped for a short break to stretch our legs and for me to catch a bathroom break. We were getting back into the vehicle when Mock closed the door on Ma Tiny's finger. He thought she had already pulled in her hand. It was painful to watch the finger begin to swell and witness the pain she was experiencing. I felt love and compassion for her fill me. I knew I loved her, would protect her, and would take the best care of her. I was of the opinion he meant to close the door on her hands, so I was angry with him until I understood it was a mistake. As I looked at the swollen finger, I got sick knowing Ma Tiny was in pain, but I also realized Mock was a good man with a good attitude.

Mock taught me how a vehicle is operated and showed me how to hook up lights by using a twelve-volt battery. Even though I was young, I never forgot anything he taught me. After two years in the Gap, it was time to come back home. The same men who had come with my father two years earlier were the crewmembers for the return trip. They got together, fixed up the boat, painted it, and made sure the ropes were strong and the blocks were working. Then they filled the drum with water and got enough food items to last us to Nassau.

Everyone was ready except me. They didn't know what was wrong with me. About two weeks before, the neighbors had given me a puppy, and I couldn't find him that morning. I didn't intend to leave him. He was very special to me. When the family told me I could choose which puppy I wanted, I was unable to make an instant choice. They were all beautiful, but as I looked them over, I saw a brown one that didn't have a tail, only a nook. I chose him and named him Rip. He was my favorite. I didn't take him next door. The houses were close, and I could go over to play with him and feed him. I fed him twice every day. This morning, however, when it was time to leave, I couldn't find him anywhere. My father wanted me to leave him because everyone was already on board and only waiting for us.

My stepmother had left on Bahamas Air earlier that morning so she could spend some time with relatives in Nassau before we left

16

for Turks and Caicos. We were supposed to leave on the boat at ten o'clock. I cried and searched for my puppy for about an hour and a half before I found him. By this time, my father was very mad. I'm sure if one had given him a cut he wouldn't have bled. My only concern was finding my pup. When I found him, I was the happiest man alive. I don't know what excuse my father gave the crew when we got aboard the boat, but I knew they were angry. I didn't care. I only wanted my puppy.

We left the Gap about one o'clock that afternoon. As the boat set sail, we watched our relatives and friends at the dock, waving good-bye and wondering when we would see each other again. The only way they would know we had arrived safely was via the radio station ZNS. In Nassau, we put an announcement on the radio so they would know. Then we would send another announcement to let them know we were leaving Nassau for Turks and Caicos. After that, they would only hear from us again by letter sent back on some other boat going to the Bahamas. There were no other means of communicating with them back then.

We sailed out of the creek and headed for Abaco. That night, we were caught in a storm. I think it was a thunderstorm. It rained, and lighting flashed all night. The *Altiny* sail was torn, and the boom broke. We were forced to stop on a little cay off Abaco for the night. We used a piece from the torn sail for our tent. Most of the crew didn't sleep as they were still getting wet from the rain. It was a rough night. The next day, we temporarily fixed the boom and sail and got underway. The only water we had on board was moved during the storm so it wouldn't roll down the deck, but we lost it anyhow because a rat fell in it and had a good swim. The voyage continued without any drinking water.

We sailed to Moore's Island Abaco, where we properly repaired the damaged boom and sail before going to Nassau. We had to send back to the Gap for canvas to repair the sail. Our stay in Moore's

Island was enjoyable. The people treated us like kings. One lady told my father I could stay with her, but I had to leave the dog on the boat. Well, that could never work. I didn't intend to separate from my dog.

After an eight-day stopover in Moore's Island Abaco, we began our trip for Nassau and arrived two days later. Our welcome party found it hard to believe we were still alive. They thought we were dead. What was supposed to be a three-day trip turned into nearly two weeks! Ma Tiny was glad to see me. She hugged me so tightly that I was closer to dying from that hug than I had been in the storm. She was sure glad to see me.

We stayed in Nassau for five days before leaving for home. We purchased wholesale groceries and other items to take back home, some to resell and some for relatives and friends. During my stay in Nassau, I met more of my step-aunts and uncles. Ma Tiny had the largest family I had ever seen. But I was more interested in my new puppy. He was the only one I could tell what to do and not to do. Everyone else was telling me what to do.

We had a grand tour of Nassau and visited the schools, some churches, the prison in Fox Hill, the reform school for problem children, sixty-six steps, and the lighthouse. This was all good and well, but I was ready to go back home to show off my puppy and see my friends.

We left Nassau on a Friday for Turks and Caicos, hoping to reach there by the following Friday or Saturday. Now, we had to pass the island of Providenciales to go to East Harbor to enter the country. Still no customs or immigration officers were working in Blue Hills. I thought that was one of the dumbest things that could happen to anyone. However, we did stop in Five Cays, one of the settlements in Providenciales, to let people know we were back and get water for the trip to East Harbor. We spent about two hours there before leaving for the last lap of the voyage. Everyone was glad to know we would soon be home again. We got into East Harbor and were finished after a few hours. The crew was just as ready to go home as I was, and we left.

About eleven o'clock the next morning, we arrived in Blue Hills, on the north side in front of our road. Some of the other sloops came out to meet us as we sailed in. When we dropped our anchor in the harbor, people were so glad to see us that they swam out to the boat. The children came out to see me, and to their surprise, I had a dog! At first, they didn't know I had him, but when he saw them, he began running up and down the boat deck barking with excitement. He was glad to be at his new home. As the children came near the boat, he jumped into the water with them and began swimming. I didn't know he could swim, and I was worried. I jumped in behind him, thinking I had to protect him from getting hurt or drowning. On reaching the shore, he ran the children up and down the beach, which was crowded with people singing and dancing, welcoming us home. Everyone liked Rip.

It was good to be back home and feel such a warm welcome from friends, neighbors, and well-wishers. From the beach, I walked to our yard. It was cleaned up nicely, but the house needed painting, so it looked different to me. After a few days of rest, Baba (my father) began painting the house. He did the inside and outside, which made me feel much better. For nearly a month, steady streams of visitors were coming and going constantly. Some bought groceries while others received letters from relatives and packages of used clothing. Back then, there wasn't much money on the islands or work to obtain money. People were glad to receive used clothes, or "Bang Yang," from their loved ones in the Bahamas. Family and friends in the Bahamas saved their used clothing for relatives in Turks and Caicos. Whenever a boat went over, they would send these clothes back for those who needed them. People were kind to each other then.

My parents found something for everybody who visited, including candies for the children, sodas and other drinks for the adults as they conversed. My friends were given small gifts from me, if only a singlet or vest, T-shirt, pair of pants, or shirt. Well, it wasn't from me, but from Ma Tiny on my behalf.

After several weeks, life got back to normal, but I had to adjust to the road, a footpath ankle-deep in sand, and the darkness. It was. Bushes were on both sides, so we called it the "Bush Road." After spending two long years in the Bahamas riding my bicycle or in vehicles on good roads, it was hard to become accustomed again to walking in ankle-deep sand. It was hard, especially at night, walking this dark, narrow road without feeling afraid. We lived close to the Bethany Baptist Church, and the cemetery was right in front of our house. You could imagine the feeling.

On another trip, we went to Cape Haiti. Now, there wasn't much money to purchase items with. The men got conchs and fish to carry to exchange for fruits, vegetables, corn, rum, and other items. The preparation took a month. Conchs and the scale fish had to be dried. Most of the fishing was done at West Caicos, an uninhabited island nineteen miles west of Blue Hills.

When fishing, the dingy would always have two men in it, one in the stern to scull the boat and one in the bow to hook the conch or strike the fish. The bowman used a water glass that magnified objects in the water so he could know where to hook or strike. This was really backbreaking work. He had to lean over the side of the boat while looking through his water glass. When he saw his object, he'd have to hook or strike with his other hand while still holding the water glass. Then he had to rise up, put whatever he caught in the boat, and go back again.

If he were getting conch, after taking in about two hundred, they would anchor the boat to take the conchs out of their shells. This was mainly the sculler's responsibility. A hammer-like tool, a conch knocker, was used to put a small hole in the shell.

The bowman would use a small knife, put it in the hole under the lip of the conch, and twist it a little, and the conch would slide out. The conchs were then ready to be cleaned in a process called slopping. All the parts, including the guts, were removed. A hole was placed in the topside so the conch could be placed in bundles of twenty-five. The next day, they would have to be beaten, placed in pairs on strings, and hung out to dry. During the evenings before bedtime, the men would tell each other stories of how many conch they got or how they had to maneuver not to lose one. Being in the water, the whole day made bathing unnecessary. Only a small amount of fresh water was used to rinse the skin before going to bed. The next morning, everyone was up at five thirty to begin the cycle again. Conchs from the day before were prepared for drying by being hung on a line made from the leaves of a silver top palm. These strong leaves were tied together until a long-enough line was made to hold all the conch in pairs. After enough drying, they were placed in bunches of fifty pairs called strings. This would be referred to as a "hundred conch."

On weekends, the fishermen headed back to the mainland to attend church with their families. When all this preparation for the voyage to Haiti was completed, the sloop was pulled onto the shore of the beach to be cleaned, dried, and painted. She would now not be loggy (water-soaked) and make more speed. On this trip, my father was to buy stuff for my oldest sister Francis's wedding. Her expected husband was also on the trip. He was making his wedding preparations as well.

Baba built a dingy boat just for this trip because, like other things, every ship should have a good lifeboat. He named that dingy after me, the *St. Charles*. She was my boat. I was proud of her.

We left Five Cays, sailing for East Harbor to clear customs and immigration before heading for Cape Haiti. The trip was smooth sailing the whole way. We arrived in the cape just before dark that day. By the time my father, the captain, completed the entering process into Haiti, the sun was gone. It was too late to do anything else that day. The crew went ashore, leaving my parents, my expected brother-in-law, and me on board. Baba drank then. He sent a Haitian man to buy him a bottle of Three Star Barbancourt Rum. Well, he had his wife, his son, and his rum, so it didn't matter what fun the others were having on shore. For a long time, I sat in the cabin door watching the lights and listening to some rumba music coming from La Facet. I listened until I was sleepy and watched the red and green lights on the buoy. By the time the jolly crew came back, I was in dreamland.

Very early the next morning, we all got up. It was time to get rid of the fish and conch aroma, which wasn't so good. To get goods sold in Haiti, one had to obtain an agent, so that was the first thing Baba did. He got dressed, and he was gone for about forty minutes. When he returned, he was in the company of a man, Gerald Gomez, the appointed agent. At that time, Haitian boats came to Turks and Caicos, bringing fruits and vegetables for sale. They weren't required to get agents. If any of us reminded them of that biased situation, they pretended not to understand. Of course, the authorities would have had to make that decision. After Baba handed the goods over to the agent, he took us to a restaurant for something to eat. That was the first time I ate turkey eggs. They were good. By the time we got back to the boat, all of the conch and fish were gone to De Ladvance. I didn't see any of it again.

Next, we went to one of Baba's friends, Dee Dee, one of the nicest persons I've ever met. She couldn't stop looking at me and hugging me. Because she liked me, she allowed me to drink many bottles of sodas, three and four per day. We stayed there for a whole week. You can imagine the amount of sodas I drank. That was the first time I saw a Chinese person, Dee Dee's husband. They were nice people who treated us very kindly.

We went to the iron market to buy cloth, shoes, hats, sheets, pillowcases, and whatever we needed for household purposes. We found everything there. This was the first time I saw so many people in one place, and everybody wanted something from us.

By the time we got back to Dee Dee's house, I was tired and hungry. She had already prepared food for us so we ate before we went back to the boat. She suggested I stay with her while we were there, but there was no way I was going to let Ma Tiny go back to the boat where Baba was without me.

The week went by quickly, and soon, everybody had what he wanted. We were ready to return home. The boat was loaded with bananas, plantain, oranges, mangoes, potatoes, yams, eddies, grits, corn, syrup, rice, vegetables, dry salted beef and pork, cherry brandy, sodas, and monkey bag. I suppose we had everything in food and drinks that we could find in Haiti. After everything was stowed away, the dinghys were strapped to the mast with one on each side of the boat for proper balancing. Dee Dee gave me six cases of sodas, five gallons of syrup, six chickens, two turkeys, and some other stuff I can't remember. These my father stowed in the *St Charles*. We waved good-bye to everyone on the dock and were on our way. Boats always left Haiti after four o'clock in the afternoon because the land breeze would die and the sea breeze would blow strong enough for the boat to make good time on the ocean. Before long, we were out by Pick-o-la Mountain, sailing due north.

As we traveled the channel on our northward course, we suddenly heard a big wave coming toward us. Ma Tiny was sitting in the cabin door, and I was right behind her, getting the warmth from the cabin. Several men were sitting on the stern when the wave hit. For what seemed an hour, but might have been only a minute, we were underwater.

When the men gained their composure and realized we were still alive, Baba asked Ma Tiny, "Tiny, where is Charlie?"

She replied, "I got him by his foot. Grab him quick! Quick!"

My head and most of my body were overboard and underwater. I learned to appreciate my big feet then. If it weren't for my big foot for her to have something to hold, I would have been history. They got me on board and inquired about everybody else. Someone called out that all were aboard except for James.

"Jesus, what is this?" Ma Tiny said.

It was dark. We had no light of any kind, and this man was adrift in the middle of the ocean. We had to turn back to look for him. Heavily loaded with necessities for the inhabitants of Providenciales, we turned her around, sailing in the opposite direction for about five minutes.

Then we heard someone saying, "Over here."

It was James. The one dinghy left with a plank knocked out was thrown overboard. With a bucket from the hatch and two oars, they maneuvered it in the direction of the voice. After a few minutes groping in the dark, they returned to the vessel with James. Everyone thanked God he was found and that we didn't sink.

The *St. Charles* was gone with everything on board. I had been so proud of it. I cried. The sloop boom was broken and the sail was torn so we couldn't make any speed. Some of the crewmembers suggested we turn back to Haiti, but Baba thought we were closer to home. It made sense to try to reach home. He was of the opinion that, if we continued, we would be close the next day. We sailed all night with big waves knocking the boat from side to side.

At the break of day, the men began to feel better, and we all felt improved after the sunrise. We were unable to cook because the waves had washed our galley, water, and everything overboard. The crew wanted to fix the broken boom, but then realized they had no tools. So we drifted without making much progress until about ten o'clock.

All of a sudden, we saw a big sail heading straight for us coming from the northwest. Now we felt better. In about ninety minutes, that boat was close enough for us to see each person and talk to each other.

That was the *KCM Orlando*. Captain W. L. Swann was on his way to East Harbor and Grand Turk to pick up passengers and clear immigration and customs for a voyage to the Bahamas. They were considered the mail boat between Turks and Caicos and the Bahamas. They told us, when they saw the boat so far south, they figured it was the *Altiny* because they were expecting us, so they came to our rescue. They tied the *Altiny* astern the *KCM Orlando* while Gus Lightbourne, another fine boat builder, along with the crew from the *KCM Orlando*, fixed the boom and everything else that needed repairs. They were equipped with tools, pieces of wood, and extra canvas. We provided foodstuff so a meal was prepared while the boat was being repaired. Those men who drank even got a bottle of monkey bag. The captain and crew of the *KCM Orlando* spent the whole day with us, making sure we were set before they left. We said our good-byes. She went south; we went north. By this time, the sun was almost down. We didn't see the *KCM Orlando* until about eleven o'clock the next day. They couldn't believe we had gotten to East Harbor before them.

We arrived about eight thirty that morning. The *Altiny* was really a fast boat. We stayed in East Harbor that whole day, collecting items we couldn't or didn't get in Cape Haitian. We got salt, lard, and flour. The next morning at six, we set sail for Providenciales. About five thirty that evening, we dropped anchor at our road. We didn't off-load the cargo that night but left two crewmembers on board, along with a couple friends who watched the boat for us. Again, we received a very warm welcome. The inhabitants had already heard by radio that Captain Swann had helped us and we were well. Cable and Wireless, a telephone company, had the only form of communication between the islands. People went to the station and paid for their announcements to be put on so their relatives would know what was happening. At that time, telephones were only on Grand Turk, so if a government official or doctor were about to visit, this announcement would be placed on the radio to notify people concerned in the Caicos Islands. The radio owners would let the others know just what was happening.

Early the next morning, the cargo was off-loaded. People came from the three settlements to purchase food items or whatever they needed. The people from the Bight came by boat since this was easier than walking or riding donkeys. The people from Five Cays had to walk the narrow, rocky roads. These roads went uphill and down valleys for about three hours, a very tiresome journey. At the end of it, a nice, soft bed would be ideal. We sold everything besides the sodas and monkey bag that we had brought for my sister's wedding, which was to take place in three weeks. After nearly everything was sold, the *Altiny* was put on the beach to be dried out and painted. During this week, the men would meet at their favorite place and talk about their bravery coming from Haiti. Pretty soon, these beautiful trips would come to an end.

In my childhood, I heard about hurricanes, especially the 1945 hurricane that took so many lives in the Caicos Islands. My father told me stories about that hurricane that I will never forget. They were out in the boat as usual because they supported their families that way. They were getting conchs and noticed it was getting dark but paid no attention to it because they thought it was going to rain.

They weren't very concerned, especially because it was so calm. They took their time getting back to the sloop. Some of the dinghys with men in them were lost. Baba was among those who got back to the boat. Before they were able to get underway and head for the mainland, they were experiencing winds of one hundred miles per hour. They were only able to get another anchor and try to stabilize the sloop before they headed below to endure the storm. Eleven days later, they found themselves on Acklins Island in the Bahamas. Some were too weak to move. Nine crewmembers made it back to the boat. The rest is history. The storm was so strong that they had to chop the mast out of the boat to help keep it balanced. My father said that, after ten days had passed, they were so hungry and thirsty that many weird thoughts began to fill their minds. They thought they would lose their sanity. One of the men got a big knife and sharpened it well. They began to think they would kill the smallest man first so they could have something to eat. Just before all made that decision, they saw land, a welcome sight that brought them back from cannibalism to civilization. The sight of land gave them endurance and a willingness to wait for a few more hours.

Because the boat was drifting, it ran into a reef. This reef was also close to the shore, so the men who were stronger helped the weaker ones to get to shore. On the beach, they looked around, not knowing where they were. Still depending on the stronger ones, it was decided that three of them would go look for food for the group. As the three walked away, they looked for markers that would help them find the others on returning. As they walked away and began rambling, they came upon a stream of freshwater that a donkey had fallen into. The donkey was already dead maybe for a day or so. But these men closed their eyes to sanitation and literally, in the sight of the dead animal, drank some water. Remember now, they hadn't had fresh water for eleven days. They continued to walk until they came upon a footpath, which they followed until they came upon two men returning home from the field. They told their story to these men, who gave them ripe bananas they were carrying and invited them home.

They prepared food, hot tea, drinking water, some energetic donkeys, and men who were willing to travel back with them. The other two men off the boat wanted to rest. They didn't want to go back to the beach that evening. But my father said his younger brother was one of those men out there so nothing would stop him from going back to take care of him. They found out that this was the island of Acklins. The people they met told them the name of the island and how they were situated in relation to the Turks and Caicos Islands. They stayed there for a few days until everyone was well again. The commissioner sent a sloop to take them home to Blue Hills. They were shocked to see and hear about all the damage that hurricane had done. So many men lost their lives. They knew some of these men very well. In fact, their own families thought they were dead too. They were very surprised to see them come home.

I had my own experience in 1960 when Hurricane Donna came. I was ten years old. At that time, more people had radios so everyone knew the news of a hurricane threatening. Cable and Wireless West Indies LTD kept us informed. I was in school as the excitement grew among my schoolmates. We were expecting this hurricane excitedly. We couldn't think about anything else. After listening to the latest report, the teacher informed us that we had to go home immediately. She told us not to stop on the road to play but go straight home.

When I got home, Ma Tiny was packing up clothes, baking bread, and preparing for the arrival of the storm. She instructed me to bring in all the tubs and buckets and secure anything the wind could cause to blow about. Baba was on the boat putting down extra anchors and making sure it was as secure as possible. As we quickly worked, we listened to all the instructions and updates that were given. Different places were named as shelters, including schools, churches, and private homes. We asked Mr. Livingston Swann to take shelter at his house, but we spent the night at home.

At about six thirty the next morning, the wind was so strong that it woke me up. But Baba never went to bed. Ma Tiny had already prepared as best she could for the worst, so she made tea for us with water she had heated and saved in a thermos. We ate bread quickly while we made ready to go to Mr. Swann's house.

Baba went on the beach and checked the boat again. By now, the waves were coming on the Bush Road. Baba took some linen, pillows, and extra clothes to the shelter and came back for food items. The storm was really on now. He had to crawl on his hands and knees so the wind couldn't carry him away. Before he got back to the house, we left. Ma Tiny was holding my hand, trying to get to Mr. Swann's house. A puff of wind came and threw us in a cactus plant. We had stickers all over us. Baba only found us because he heard me crying. To this day, I am convinced that he only tried to come back because of us. By now, it was really bad. Walking close together, never letting go of each other, and trying to reach safety as quickly as possible, we finally got to the house.

Then it began to rain. The wind blew harder and harder. They paid attention to the doors and windows, making sure they were safe. I must confess that that day and night was the first time I heard so much singing and praying. About 1 a.m. in the morning, the wind stopped blowing, but the rain was still pouring. Everyone stayed inside until the rain stopped later. Most of the men went outside, thinking the hurricane was over. They wanted to inspect the damages and check on the sloops. Nine were anchored off in the harbor before the storm began. These men hoped they would all be there, but they could only find one sloop. The men knew, if these boats were not completely destroyed, they were badly damaged.

The wind had begun to blow hard again, about eighty miles an hour. The storm had passed and turned back from Cuba to attack us again and then continued on a northerly course. At times, the house would shake so violently that it felt like it would move off the foundation. The kitchen had already blown away. At one point, the men went out and used heavy lumber to secure the roof since it was feeling like it would come off with all the wind. The next day after the storm was over, pieces of people's houses were in the sea, dinghy boats were in backyards, big trees had fallen everywhere, and water had settled everywhere. Baba went to check on our house, and he found the kitchen gone and some zinc off the roof. Still, we went home and started our repairs. First, we fixed the doors, got pieces of zinc, and closed the holes in the roof. Then we had to get a carpenter, Mr. Algernon Dean, to fix the planks in the dinghy boat that were knocked out. He made it look like new.

A pond was in front of our house. I swam in it for weeks because it had so much water. Water had settled everywhere. Some people had to use dinghy boats on the land to get from place to place. Drinking water became a problem because the water was salty, but this didn't last too long because it soon rained. Then we got good drinking water. We caught rainwater in buckets or sixty-gallon drums. I was mostly saddened because the *Altiny* was gone. About a month later, Baba found some pieces of her on the bottom of the sea, and some parts drifted ashore. I decided then that I hated hurricanes.

I thought to myself, *No more trips for our family.*

Baba was an unhappy man too. The *Windell* was the only boat that rode out the storm. Mr. Wilfred Rigby owned her. When they found the *KCM Orlando*, she had broken away from her mooring and ended up on the beach in the Bight.

The *Sea Fan*, Mr. Hilly Ewing's boat, was in the Bahamas at that time, so they brought food and clothing for the inhabitants. Ships were also sent with needed food items and other necessities from neighboring countries directed by Her Majesty's Government after a number of weeks. These food, clothes, toiletry, and cleaning agents were badly needed and greatly appreciated. When the ships reached Grand Turk, the officials used salt boats and sent relief to the Caicos Islands.

⚜

My father began to work as crew on the *Sea Fan* for a few trips to the Bahamas after his boat was destroyed. The voyage would begin with getting conchs to take to the Bahamas for sale. Sometimes, those trips would take long, and I would miss Baba. During those times, I would experience grave difficulty with my stepmother. She had many friends, but we spent much time with this particular family. We would often spend the night at their house, and then they would spend the night with us. There were two children in this family whose parents thought they were better than everyone else. They were especially better than I was since I didn't know who my father was. I was just nothing compared to them. A nobody!

My father built chicken coops with my help. Back then, most people raised chickens and pigs. These were our main meat at meals, especially on Sundays or if we were having guests. Some people also raised cows and goats. These were used for food too.

On Mondays, in preparation for the next Sunday, Ma Tiny would have me put two chickens in the coops and keep them there for the whole week so they could get cleaned up. We would only feed them corn and clean water. If they were left out, they could pick and eat anything that wasn't clean. Some neighbors didn't have latrines for proper sanitation, and the chickens would wander off to find food. There was no telling what they might consume.

On Sunday morning, I would be awakened early, as usual, to begin my chores, which included killing and cleaning the chickens. I always made sure the feet were cleaned properly because that was what I would get for my portion, especially if Ma Tiny's friend's children showed up for dinner.

They could choose which part of the chicken they would have. If I ever did that, she would tell me how much I could beg, or she might just slap me in my mouth. If these children were spending the night, they got the best bed with warm covers. One time, I figured, since

31

we were the same age, I could join them in the bed, but that was a mistake. I always ended up in another room sleeping on a crocus sack with dirty clothes under my head for a pillow. When Ma Tiny woke me in the mornings to go for water or wood, she would allow them to sleep while she prepared their breakfast. Sometimes, she actually fed them like babies and gave them their milk in baby bottles.

They would return to bed and suck their milk. During bath time, they could use as much water as they wanted. I was made to heat water for them so they could take warm baths. When I finished my chores about a quarter to nine, she would put three cans of water in the tub, instructing me to wash my dirty skin before going to school. By that time, the others had long since left for school with their mother walking along with them.

Baba brought some light blue paint from the Bahamas, and I painted the house. He also brought some other decorations. I always felt like we had the best house in North Side. To a certain extent, I felt rich, even though I worked very hard and was treated like a slave.

On one of the trips to the Bahamas, Baba started bringing lumber to build a new boat. Since he was on someone else's boat, he couldn't bring a lot at one time. We didn't have a storeroom, so we fixed it up in the back of the house, and Ma Tiny and I had to watch it. One night, she decided to sleep at her friend's house. The next day when we came home, the lumber wasn't there. When I reached home from school, she was crying. When I found out why, I began crying too. We knew we were in trouble if we didn't find it.

Well, I don't believe in witchcraft, or obeah, but I think it is real. At least, according to this story. A lady in Blue Hills was originally from North Caicos. She was out working one day until she got hungry and thirsty. Then she went home. After she had eaten, she picked up a glass of water someone had set on the table before she came home and drank it all. From then on, she was known to have an evil spirit. This water was set to kill someone else. It didn't kill her because it wasn't her dose. But she was messed up badly. At a certain season, she would just change from the normal person she was and become monstrous. Men used to have to hold her down to control her. During these times, she could tell fortunes or know things other people wouldn't be able to know. The voice that came through her was a man's voice. People called him Matilda. People would come from all over the island to find out things they wanted to know when he was controlling her. It used to last for some days. She owned a donkey, Moon Shine, and she burned coal for a living.

My stepmother sent me in the woods with this lady to with her to bring back some coal for us. This was just after we missed the lumber. She used to burn coal in a place called Davy Bight, about eight miles from where we lived. I could ride the donkey, so I was glad to go. It was like giving me a break from the normal chores I did daily. When we got there, she instructed me to help her fill the crocus sacks with the coal. I didn't mind because it was different from all the tasks at home. Suddenly, I noticed her looking in the bushes, and she began working quickly. She kept looking in a certain patch of bushes and worked faster. I excused myself to go in the back to take a number one.

She told me, "Don't go far, and don't stay too long."

I wasn't afraid of her, however, and I knew there was something strange about her.

Soon, she told me, "Get on the donkey." She strapped a big sack of coal on its back. "Go straight home as fast as you can, and don't stop off anywhere."

Well, there wasn't anywhere to stop anyway until I reached my mother's house in Corinize. It was a long way off. I could only stop for a drink of water from a rock hole. While I was passing Corinize, the place where I was born and where my mother lived at that time,

I felt something like a whirlwind pass me. I wondered what it was, but couldn't figure it out. I continued home, riding the donkey right up in our yard. I took the coal off, gave the donkey some water, and decided to take the donkey home. It was about ninety minutes before sunset.

This lady's house was about a mile and a half from my house. When I arrived, many people were there. I tied the donkey near a piece of green grass and tried to get in the house to find out what was happening. I knew I had left her in Davy Bight. To my amazement, there she was, lying on the floor with an enormous stomach like a pregnant woman. I just didn't want to believe my eyes.

The people around her were singing a chorus, "Satan, go away and let Jesus come in." Then I heard it for the first time, a loud man's voice coming out of her.

"Charlie, you were scared when I pass you, eh?"

I realized the weird sound I heard and felt was her and Matilda. The next afternoon, we went to her house again. It was amazing to watch her eat when the evil spirit was present. When she said she was hungry, they would get about ten quarts of corn, crack it, put it in a large bucket, and add water. She would swallow it down like a hog, but only faster. When he wasn't present, she would be normal. But when he entered her, she would make a simple kick, and her appearance would change. Strong men were usually on hand to handle her. I saw her carrying six strong men on her back. After he had entered and her stomach was increased to its maximum, she would quiet down. Then people would speak to Matilda. If at any time she happened to get away, no one could run as fast as she could. She usually stopped in the cemetery among the tombs or climb up in a tree.

She got away one time, and no one could find her. I had two good dogs, so I was asked to go with them along with others to search for her. They brought a piece of her clothing for the dogs to smell. The first time the dogs stopped, it was a cat up in a tree, so we allowed them to smell the item of clothing again. This time, they didn't stop until they found her. She was outside an old lady's house, just lying on the sand. This old lady was the popular C. Smith. She (C. Smith), was an old music teacher who was very kind to all. She was also an animal lover and always kept a dog as her companion.

When they got her back home again, we heard the voice again loudly, "Tiny, are you worrying about the lumber? Well, go further in the back. Boy Palmer hid it from you trying to fool you." Someone asked him about the whereabouts of the *Sea Fan*, Mr. Hilly Ewing's boat. It was on its way from Nassau. He said to them, "Wait a few minutes." At that time, her stomach went flat. After about ten to twelve minutes, she made a little kick, and then her stomach grew big again. He began speaking. "They were passing Long Island. Thomas Palmer is steering, and the rest are eating." Two days later, the boat reached home.

The people couldn't wait to ask them where they were that night at about nine thirty. When they said off Long Island, the people were amazed. They remembered a bird being on the mast also and concluded that that was Matilda. That same night, we went home, got a lantern, and went out to the back of the house looking for the lumber. It was in the back, hidden in the bushes just a little further from where we had hidden it first. I would never forget the look on Ma Tiny's face. She was really happy to find it.

Boy Palmer was my uncle, my father's younger brother. He was named after his father, Joseph Palmer. I think he should have been called Junior. I don't know why they called him Boy Palmer. He had passed the house two days in a row and found no one home, so on the second day, he decided to make it safe so no one could steal it. In fact, that's what he wanted Ma Tiny to think, and she certainly did. After we found it, we didn't bother to move it. We left it there for safekeeping. A few days later, the old man came home. He bought more lumber, okim, rope, paint, and stuff for Ma Tiny and me. We were glad to see him, and he was happy to be back home with his family.

After a few weeks, they began planning for another voyage. When they had enough conchs, they were on their way again. Every time my father left, my stepmother would go to her friend's house. Besides the friend's own children, two more children were living with her. These children did all of the work around the house and yard. During our stay there, I would be sent with these children to help with whatever they were doing. While we were working, if the friend's children felt like visiting us, they would walk outside, stand and watch us, and then laugh at us scornfully. At nights, we didn't sleep in the main house. We slept in the back of an older house adjacent to it, much like a barn house. We slept on crocus sacks with a few sheets over them. No pillows were allowed out there, so we slept with our heads on our arms. But the boys were nice to me. Even up to this day, the one who is still alive respects me. He married one of my first cousins.

If school was open, my stepmother would wake me up early to go home to prepare for school. She had started treating me badly and would beat me for any simple thing. After her friend's children found this out, they would tell her stories about me to watch me get punished. On one occasion, she told me to go to her friend's house with the children when school was finished. Of course, I didn't mind because that was the only time I would get to have fun. We went to their house, changed our clothes, and went down to their grandparents' yard to pick coconuts. No one told me anything about going swimming, so I wasn't prepared. I wasn't wearing any underwear. In those days, I only had underwear for church and school, and at other times, I had to leave them off and wear my yard clothes. So when my friend asked me about going swimming, I told him no.

In the grandparents' yard, there were plenty of girls, and everyone except me was ready to go swimming. I thought I shouldn't be expected to go naked, so I just sat on the beach and watched. When it was time to go back to their house, my so-called friend started running and licking his hand to form a whip. Its sound told me that he was going to tell on me. He knew, if he told Ma Tiny I did anything, she would believe him and beat me without question. I wanted to walk slowly, but I knew she would be mad, so I walked swiftly and reached the house about a minute behind him. He had already reported his story by the time I arrived.

Ma Tiny was at the door, waiting for me to bring my "you know what" to her.

She said, "I'll find out if you're a man."

She pulled down my pants and searched me good. She probably thought she saw evidence that I was getting to be a big boy that made her mad. She grabbed the broomstick and started beating me over my head. By that time the girls reached home and I was there without my pants, naked. These children stood there and watched me get a beating while they pointed at me in great outbursts of laughter. I will never forget that moment.

I was humiliated beyond words. At one point, I raised my hands toward my head to block the licks going to my head. One of the licks took on my right thumb! Everything went numb in my right hand and arm. All this time, no one told my stepmother to stop, not even the man of the house. I was looking for him to rescue me. That, however, didn't happen. He stayed in the house and pretended not to hear what was going on. His nephew, on the other hand, got tired of seeing me mistreated in that way. Hearing my screams, he grabbed my pants off the floor and pulled me away from Ma Tiny. He then walked me a little way up the road toward our house, even though he knew no one was home. He did that just to get me away from her. He carried me halfway and suggested I tried finding my way and someone to help me. I tried to creep along the beach. My legs were weak and cramping. My body was in pain. I must have passed out on the beach because, when someone woke me, it was midnight.

I was at the neighbor's house seeking attention for my thumb and hand. The thumb was broken so they put it between two flat pieces of wood. No doctors were here at that time. We went to South Caicos when we needed to see a doctor, but my grandmother was very good with her bush medicine. She tried her best for family, friends, and the entire community. When I woke up a short time afterward, my mother was standing over me crying, so I cried too. Later, someone from the house went to call Ma Tiny, but she didn't come. She stayed next door in her house because she heard my mother's voice saying what she would do her if she came in that yard. I believe that was the only time they were angry at each other because they lived like two sisters.

This neighbor, Annalee Robinson, was the mother of my mother's husband, the one who had left her for so long. But during that whole ordeal, she never severed the relationship with my mother. They remained close. She always walked along the beach when she went anywhere. That's how she found me. I was lying there out like a light. She said she called my name, but I didn't answer. I couldn't. The pain was unbearable. She carried me on her back to her house. She was a short woman but very strong. I didn't eat all day because, after school, we went down in the yard to pick coconuts, so I was very hungry by that time. I ate at about one o'clock that morning after I woke up.

This happened on a Friday afternoon. On Saturday morning, Ma Tiny came into the neighbor's yard, but not in the house. She was crying and pleading to my mother to let me come home with her, saying she was so sorry for what she did and confessing that she didn't know my finger was broken. During those days, people were very cruel to children. Before I passed out on the beach, I could hear the boy who helped me crying because his uncle was beating him for helping me escape. He told me he knew he would get punished because he pulled me away from her. His uncle was telling him that he had disrespected Ma Tiny because he pulled me away from her.

I felt sorry for him as I heard his cries, "Don't kill me, Baba Joe. Please don't kill me with that cow cock."

My mother didn't let me go home with Ma Tiny that day. Instead, she took me home with her. I wanted to be with my mommy, but I didn't like Corinize. Up there, it seemed too dark, and there were too many night noises, including the crickets. My father got home about eleven that morning and heard about the story before he secured his dinghy boat. He left everything and went to talk to Ma Tiny but didn't find her. She was hiding. She saw him, but he didn't see her. He secured his boat, cleaned himself up, and came to my mother to see me. He took one look at me and began to cry. However, he asked me to tell him the story as it happened. He then asked my mother if she had anything in the "bitters bottle." The bitters bottle consisted of different roots steeped in monkey bag, better known as "claran." Two drinks of that mixture made people act and feel differently. He began to swear that he was going to kill that woman whenever he found her. Even though she had beaten me sick, broken my finger, and killed my self-esteem, I loved her and didn't want him to kill her. You see, I knew Emily was my mother, but the love wasn't there like it was for Ma Tiny. Maybe, as a toddler, when I first realized a woman was caring for me, it was Ma Tiny. The love for my mother came later through the years.

My father said to my mother, "Let Charlie go with me." She said "No." So he said, "Then I will stay with him." He asked me, "Do you want to go home with me?" I said "Yes." Mommy decided to let me go since I wanted to. By this time, she had finished cooking dinner, so she fed us. We were ready to leave. The bitters bottle was now nearly empty. We started on our journey. My father picked me up and put me around his neck, and he carried me until we reached the Bush Road. He put me down to light a cigarette and took a smoke. When he finished, he picked me up again and carried me all the way home.

When we got there, we could smell bread baking, so we knew she was home. We still didn't have an oven in the house, so she was baking in the outside oven in the back of the house and didn't know we had arrived. At the same time, she came from the back of the house, so he caught up with her. I was sorry for her that evening. I was still in pain. My finger, hand, and arm were hurting, but I had to tell my father not to beat her like that. When he somewhat stopped, I ran and held her, and we went outside in the backyard. When he cooled down later, I went back into the house, got some sheets and pillows, checked the oven to make sure the fire wasn't too high under the bread, and then went back where she was hiding. We found some grass, spread the sheets, and lay down. I lay deep in thought until I fell asleep.

The next morning, Sunday, I woke up in the house. I don't know how I got there. Many people came to see me after church. I was unable to go to school for a long while. My stepmother was good to me for a few months, at least until I was healed up. After that, she started working me hard again in the fields, bringing water, and cleaning the yard. Wherever there was work, I was present. We had five fields at that time: two in the Sam Bay area we called Guze, two in Mary Hill called N.W.& N. Central, and one behind the house. These fields kept us busy with not much time for school. My father began building another boat around that time too. He would wake me early each morning to cut timber in the bushes for the new boat. We always cut three pieces. He brought two while I would bring one and the axe.

Even though I had to work, I was glad when he was home because I got to go to school on time. When we got back from cutting timber, he would make sure I got breakfast and prepared for school. I enjoyed going to school because that was the only time I had for meeting friends, playing marbles, and climbing sapodilla and tamarind trees.

The short time I spent in school was enjoyable. My teachers even became more understanding after they found out that my stepmother used to wait for the big gray flag to go down before she sent me to school. When the head mistress asked her why, her excuse was that I would play too much if I went early. She never thought I would be more relaxed and ready to learn if I went in time. Education wasn't important to her, work was all that mattered, and no one could change her mind.

After Baba had cut enough timber, he employed Mr. Gus Lightbourne, a fine boat builder, to start building. He had built several big boats in his time and some of the fastest, including the *KCM Orlando*, the *Gracie J*, the *Lady Foot*, the *Federation*, and the *General Express*. One morning, he started chopping timber to shape the boat bow and stern. I was very anxious to see the boat finished, but in those days, everything was done using mere muscles. There were no gasoline or electrical powered anything. All tools were manual, so you could imagine how long it took to build a boat thirty-eight feet long. Some weeks, my father would stay on land to help Gus work on the boat.

During those times, life wasn't so hard for me. Ma Tiny would still, as always, feed me last, but I didn't worry about it because Baba always left food on his plate for me. He never ate everything off his plate unless he was away from home. When he was away in the boat, I could still always stop at Mrs. Kathleen Lightbourne's house when I went to the well, and she would give me dinner. She was married to Gus Lightbourne. She was a nice lady. Sometimes she came to watch Mr. Lightbourne at work on the boat and notice how hard I worked, never stopping to eat. She had two sons, Tom and Cheese, my best friends. In fact, we lived like brothers. We did many things together, especially Cheese and me.

It was the hardest pill to swallow when I heard of his death. Crying and loud noises broke the silence of the night. I tried to get up and remembered I couldn't because of the wound from the accident to my left leg. So I lay in bed wondering what had happened. Shortly afterward, someone came and told us that Cheese had just gotten knocked down and the driver hadn't stopped. It seemed impossible. "Cheese just got killed!" I was very disappointed I couldn't go out to be there for the family.

I had been involved in an accident that had wounded my leg and hip a few days earlier. I was out delivering water when the truck, filled with water, rolled over, and my left leg got trapped under it. This was my first major accident, and I was scared. I was glad the engine was already turned off because a fire might have occurred. My helper, a bigger man than I was, fell on me. I had to help him up and out of the other side so he could call for help. I was praying someone was listening on the vhf (very high frequency radio), so he could be understood because he was tongue-tied. But he was heard and understood right away.

He also broke the windshield so I could get air. As soon as he called for help, many people started coming to the scene to see what happened, some out of curiosity and others out of concern. The crowd of onlookers soon became larger as the news spread. Mr. Art Butterfield knelt beside me and encouraged me to hold on. When he stood up again, he prayed that help would come soon. The accident happened in Johnston's yard, and Johnston's equipment came to remove the truck so I could be free. The machine was doing a job in South Dock, about seven or eight miles away. The road was still rough, but I fancy everything was done in record time. About ninety minutes later, I was free and headed for the clinic. Dr. Euan Menzies, our family doctor, was also called to the scene. He was on hand to attend to me on the spot. He and Dr. Sam Slattery tended to me for days after I went home. The bone specialist, Dr. Jack Cooper, whom

I attended in Miami for further treatment, commended these doctors highly. He thought they did a very good job.

I am grateful for the miracle that their expertise helped to perform. I recognize that God loves me! My leg wasn't broken; neither was there a fractured bone. The insurance company thought my leg was a risk and said they couldn't cover it, but many years have passed, and I am still on that leg, strong as ever. Thanks be to God!

I am very glad someone heard Boy Dean's cry for help and came to my rescue. It was a very hard pill for me to swallow when I couldn't even attend Cheese's funeral because I was away seeking medical attention.

Finally, the boat was finished. On the morning of the launch, I was excited. My parents sent me to school with instructions to come home when class went out for lunch. My mind was on what was happening at home. I don't think I concentrated on anything else that day. I told my teachers I had to leave, and they gave me permission to do so. I left quickly and ran all the way up the beach until I reached the boat. They had already made straps of ropes and placed rollers under the keel, making it ready to slide into the water. A big crowd was gathering to help with the launching. When my stepmother saw me, she sent me home to change out of my school clothes and come back. By the time I got back, everyone was holding the ropes, pulling and singing this song, "Young girl, Liza, ready for the water. Heave away! Heave away!" The boat started moving.

She was painted white at the top and red at the bottom with blue trimming. The deck was gray. Many different color flags were all over and around her. She was beautiful. The men were happily laughing and fixing the skids under the boat so she could keep rolling. When she was almost to the water, my stepmother got up on the deck. Someone handed her something in a white pillowcase—two bottles of rum. They told her to hold on tight as they pulled on the ropes again. When the boat was in the water, Ma Tiny burst the bottles on the side of the boat. That made a loud sound, and liquid flew everywhere. During this process, Ma Tiny named the boat the SS *Wheeland Queen*. People began dancing, celebrating this wonderful day with our family.

When they took the boat far out enough for her to float, she was straight and tall in the water. Someone shouted that she wasn't cranky and Gus had done a fine job. My father always took pride in what he did, and this was no exception. He was proud of his accomplishment. The boat was painted nicely and with all new fixtures. To get the boat far out enough to anchor her, they used two staffs about twelve feet long, one on either side pushing against the shallow seabed to move her along, and finally secured her to her mooring. Everyone went to our house to eat, dance, and get drunk. Most of the people went home later in the evening, but some were too drunk to move.

Early the next morning, Baba got up and went on the beach to look at her anchored in front of his landing. I could see the joy in his face. Then I realized the *Altiny* was off his mind. Later that day, some of the men who had asked him to pull their dinghy boat came to help rig the boat up and make her ready for her first voyage. On my way up from school, I could see the mast standing up on the SS *Wheeland Queen*. I felt bigger than my old man did. Two days later, it was time for the test. With everything in place, we were ready to see her sail. The men filled some sacks with sand to make ballast. For good ballast, we would usually use pebbles from South Caicos. So until that trip was made, sand was substituted.

Everything was checked: the sail, mast, boom, and pump. All were good. They even checked for water, but that boat was as dry as a bottle and looked picture-perfect. In my excitement to see her sail, I didn't see how fast sunset was approaching. The men, however, who had worked all day, were ready to go home. When I realized they weren't sailing that evening, I was disappointed.

I thought, *If I could sail this boat myself, I would try it right now!*

Alas, I had to wait until the next morning to see the boat set sail. The men were back about ten o'clock. My father was already on the beach when they arrived. I was hurrying to catch them because I didn't want to be left behind. I wanted to be there when the boat did her first trip in the harbor.

When Baba saw me coming, he sailed toward me, shouting. "Let's go, Charlie!"

We got into a dinghy and rowed out to the sloop. We didn't have any engines in Blue Hills at that time so I was the sculler. At the boat, we jumped on board, and the dinghy was tied astern. Sails were hoisted, anchors were pulled in, and she was on her way. People wanting to see the *Wheeland Queen* sail for the first time lined the beach. We sailed up the harbor and then down. I noticed my father at the helm, smiling as he looked behind the boat at the rudder as she sailed.

I asked him, "Why are you doing that? I don't want to miss anything that is happening."

He confided, "You know a boat is sailing fast when you see the beads coming from the rudder and hear a noise like something cutting through the water."

By the movements of the people on the shore, we could tell the way the boat sailed impressed them. We delighted them many times over by sailing up and down the harbor, displaying her ability to move fast. On the last lap, three of the crewmembers took their conch shell horns and began to blow them. This exercise was to inform the other boat owners that this boat was now ready to enter a contest. For several weeks, races were held. She usually came in first and occasionally third depending on the wind. We respected this one boat, the SS *Windell*, Mr. Wilfred Rigby's vessel. She was something else! If the wind were moderate, she would beat the *Wheeland Queen*, but if we had to take in "Single Reef" in our sail, we would put distance on her. By that time, they had already found her trim.

The *Wheeland Queen* had one thing on all the other boats, beauty. She was a beautiful sight to behold. Maybe that's why she was called the *Wheeland Queen*.

My father no longer needed to get conchs or make the voyage to Haiti for food to make ends meet. The fishing plants were paying a penny a pound for lobster so he fished for lobster to sell to the fisheries. Many lobsters were on the bank then, and life began to get a little easier. My old man was on his way up again. He had a crew he could depend on now. They would sometimes go to South Caicos and fish for two weeks and then bring back groceries and other necessities. Freighters had begun to come here from the United States, bringing food and building materials. My father was now able to add a new piece to the house. I was convinced ours was the best house. Baba always painted it light blue with a red roof.

On one of those two-week fishing trips, my stepmother's friend started coming over more often. I decided they were coming so often because they thought our standard of living was getting better and they wanted to share in the good times. They didn't have a boat. On Monday morning, Ma Tiny told me to catch four roosters and put them up in the chicken coop for the week. I knew this meant she was having company. I decided the crowd would be big because of the number of chickens. I wondered what part of the chicken I would get on my plate. For the whole week, I was cleaning the house and the yard in preparation for the weekend. I went to school late and ran home quickly before the other children to avoid getting a beating. I didn't forget the last one and didn't want to come under her wrath. She still beat me for every little thing, and I didn't know why.

On Saturday morning, I was up early before six o'clock. I had to go to the wells for water, get firewood from the bushes for cooking, go to the shop for sugar to bake the bread with, and buy kerosene oil for the lamps. And then I still had to scrub the floors. The floors were wooden with no carpet, rug, or tiles, so we had to scrub often to keep the floors clean. We would walk the beach to fetch pieces of sea fan, "husker," to scrub the floor. Of course, that was my job. Later into the afternoon and evening, I helped her bake her bread. I grated the potatoes for potato bread, mixed up the batter for the gingerbread, and helped her knead the white bread. We stayed up until all the different breads were finished and then went to bed. The next day was Sunday, and Ma Tiny allowed me to sleep until six o'clock.

We met and conducted our prayer meeting or family devotion. Then she told me to kill the chickens. By now, I was getting pretty good at this job. Within a short while, I had everything cleaned and cut up the way she had showed me. I put special effort into cleaning the legs or feet because that was what I usually got. Ma Tiny began to cook before church time. She was really a good cook. Steamed chicken with peas and rice and fried plantain was her specialty.

At church, I saw her friend and her children. When the service was over, the children told me they were coming to our house for dinner. Well, I had already figured something like that, but I wasn't sure. However, I was glad to have company. Another friend and her children showed up, so I anticipated a wonderful afternoon with friends.

We changed our clothes and went outside to play while we were waiting for dinner to finish cooking. The food seemed to be taking long, and we decided to go into the house to ask for bread because we were getting hungry. I agreed to go with them, but they were the ones who could ask and get it without any problem. In fact, that was the reason she baked so much bread, so they could get what they wished.

One of the bigger girls was put in charge of cutting and distributing the bread to the others. She cut up a whole loaf of bread and buttered each slice on both sides. She then gave each child a slice except me. I watched them eat. Then the exercise began again with each child getting a second slice of buttered bread, all except me. I became hurt and angry, so I decided I would cut a slice for myself, knowing this was my father's house, my father's food, and I was my father's son. I had already washed my hands even though the others hadn't. I thought this was a plus for me. I took the bread knife in my hand to begin cutting a slice of bread for myself. I don't know yet how my stepmother got in the pantry so quickly. She came out of nowhere. I felt something hit me so hard that I thought my neck was broken. I fell down with the knife falling in one direction and the bread in the other. Then she kicked me under the table where the piece of bread had fallen. At the same time, she was shouting at me, questioning: "When did you start cutting bread in my house? Are you crazy? Stop showing off your rank self, okay!"

I felt ashamed and low. The children were all laughing at me and enjoying the insults and abuse she was giving me. When she finished, she instructed the same girl: "Give him a slice of bread, but no butter!" I really didn't have any appetite for that bread anymore, but she told me, "If you don't eat that bread, I will punish you real good." My friends were still laughing and pointing at me under the table, and I had to eat that bread to save embarrassment. Along with the bread, I had to eat my tears and snot from my nose. And there I was, thinking I was so good to wash my hands before eating when the girl in charge of the bread didn't even think about it. But what did I get? A punch, a slap, a couple kicks in my ribs, and low self-esteem.

When dinner was finally done, everyone gathered around the table for a feast. I was the only one off in a corner. Ma Tiny's best friend helped her to dish up the food. The children were allowed to choose which parts of the chicken they wanted and got them too.

I had to keep my mouth shut in the corner. I was too embarrassed to even look up at the children anymore. When everyone had what they wanted and were eating happily, only then did Ma Tiny give me an enamel plate with about a spoonful of rice mixed with the part that stuck to the pot during the cooking process (the pot cake), four chicken feet, and plenty of gravy. It looked like I was drinking soup instead of eating peas and rice. The others ate from fine china plates and drank their sodas from tumblers. My soda was put in a condensed milk can. After everyone was finished, they were allowed to relax while I cleaned up. Some threw themselves across the beds while others sat around and played. I was instructed to move the plates and glasses without breaking even one, or my head would get broken the same way. That kind of treatment went on for a long time.

We used to work the fields in a Sam Bay area we called Guze. We got out of bed at five o'clock in the morning to take the long walk out to Guze to put in a full day's work. Many times, the road was dark until sunrise. It would be dark again before we would see home. Our walk back was even more difficult because of heavy loads we carried on our heads consisting of corn, potatoes, peas, or whatever produce we had. These sacks were sometimes packed with a single item or all these items mixed, amounting to sixty or even one hundred pounds. I didn't wear shoes and sometimes would have up to three toes bursting at the same time. Of course, I didn't have time to look at them because I had to get home and shuck peas to cook for dinner.

At times, we didn't get through until midnight, and then our preparations for bed would take us to one o'clock. Five o'clock came so quickly some mornings. My body just wanted to go back to sleep. When that happened, a bucket of cold water thrown over me would wake me up. Also, I had to get to the wells early before others got there to get nice, clean water. Latecomers often had to wait until the well sprang again. My stepmother would often go back to bed until about six thirty after waking me up.

I was glad when my father decided to build a catchment, (that's a tank built to preserve rain water) later on. A hole was dug in the ground, then plastered with concrete mixture and covered with zinc panels or other roofing materials used at the time. Gutters were attached to catch the water from the roof of the house and channeled to go into the tank. I helped dig the hole with pickaxe and shovels. I later mixed concrete and helped with the construction to get it finished. Then I prayed for rain because, if it did, we would have water and I didn't have to go to the wells so early to fetch it. While working on that tank, corns covered my hands from handling the heavy tools and working so hard. I was glad though to have the pleasure of a tank in my yard. Only about seven homes on the island then had their own catchments. Most people still used a sixty-gallon drum outside to catch rainwater for drinking. Other people still got their drinking water from holes in the rock, or "Rock Hole." They would take gallon bottles or lard canisters to bring water home.

During the drought periods, we got good drinking water from the Bight wells. Men would go in boats so enough water could be brought for a number of families. Later, however, the government built a few public tanks to provide good drinking water for the whole island, including the schoolchildren. I didn't have to go to the well so early now, but that didn't stop the hard work or unreasonable demands that Ma Tiny put on me. She would send me to the shop and spit on the rock when I was leaving and inform me I had to be back before the spit dried. Since the shop was a five-mile round-trip, I had to run to avoid a beating. Then again, the sun dried the spit in no time so I got a beating anyway.

Most owners' shops were located in an extra piece built onto the house. They would be in the house doing their other work until someone came to make a purchase. Usually a dog or family of dogs was in the yard, and children sent by parents to make purchases would stand well out of reach and call until someone heard them. Sometimes, if they thought one was calling too much, they would drive you away from their yards so they could do their work in contentment. I always ended up late but was never allowed to explain why. I think Ma Tiny's favorite pastime was to beat me.

My father wasn't true to his marriage vows. He kept many other women and didn't spend much time at home. Sometimes he would come home when he was finished working, eat his dinner, bathe, and leave for hours at a time. He wasn't an attractive man, but a real lover in which regard my brother Mackie takes after him. I concluded that Ma Tiny was constantly mad with my father so she took it out on me, conjuring up any reason to punish me. She would summon me to the table with my books to do my lessons to see if I was learning anything. Other times, I would know I was spelling a word correctly, and she would believe it wrong and beat me anywhere on my body: my legs, sides, back, belly, or face. When I finally made it to bed, my body would be sore all over. Many times, I tried to duck the special, red, razor-sharp belt she kept especially to beat me with, but she was quicker than I was. I have scars I will carry to my grave from the many beatings I got from her with that particular belt.

I had the most fun when she allowed me to go to Corinize to spend time with my mother and get acquainted with my cousins. I had freedom then. We used to go looking for sea grapes, sapodillas, tamarind, bird's eggs, and whatever else we chose to do.[1]

We often walked along the beach looking for coconuts or anything we thought valuable that drifted up on the shore. When we were among the trees and bushes, we often made accidental contact with wasp nests and returned home with our eyes swollen from all the stings. We had many good times together, especially with my cousin Theophilus Williams (Tee). He always wore a brown outfit so the children teased him and called him the "Gingerbread Man." They would take his lunch from him, maybe eat some, and then throw the rest away. Mommy used to fix our lunch before we left for school. Now Tee couldn't fight, so I had to fight for him, but he was strong. If we were fighting two or three boys, I would let him hold one while I fought with the other two. If they were bigger, I would take them on one at a time, maybe one today and the other the next, but I always got them.

When it was time to go back home, the thoughts of hard work would surface. At Corinize, the work was never so hard, and my cousins always helped me with what little I had to do. With them, I thought I had it made. The only drawback was at night. Corinize was too dark. I had nightmares there, and I was afraid to go to sleep. It always seemed darker than at home, where, even with the cemetery only two hundred feet away, I wasn't scared. And when I did at last get to go to bed, I was contented.

---

1 A sapodilla is an evergreen tree having latex that yields chickle, a coagulated milky juice used today as the principal ingredient of chewing gum, and edible fruit called naseberry with sweet yellow-brown flesh. Tamarind is a tropical Asian evergreen tree having leaves resembling a feather, pale yellow flowers, and thick cinnamon brown pods containing an edible pulp. The fruit of this tree was eaten fresh or used in the preparation of chutney, curry, or even soft drinks.

At Corinize, my stomach was always full though, sometimes too full. My cousins called me to have food when their parents cooked, and Mommy was feeding me as well. I missed that kind of treatment when I returned home. Ma Tiny would remind me by saying she hoped I enjoyed my rest because the work was still there waiting for me to get it done. The cycle started all over again. I worked so hard and missed everything like holidays and picnics for many years.

When it was time to weed the fields, we would go to Sam Bay for the week. A camp was already built to stay in. It was thatched with a floor made of grass. Our route into Guze from the beach took us past the exact spot where Crystal Bay Resort is now located. We would pass by there to the other side of the island where the fields were. We would leave for the field early, and by the time we got there, I was ready for a long nap, but alas, it was time to work.

Weeds were pulled from among the growing produce. Hired men cut down more trees to enlarge the field. As the day grew older, I would be instructed to go to the rock hole for water to cook with. When I finished, I would shuck peas and cut up okra for the soup. Dry conchs were common back then, so there would be conchs to soak along with the salt beef or pigtails. Then I would have to dig potatoes to add to the soup. In the evening after dinner, I would find some water to wash my face and feet before going to bed. After working all day, everyone slept deeply from exhaustion. I, on the other hand, couldn't go to sleep because of my fear of rats running about nearby. I feared they would come near me or touch me. So I got little sleep and came to hate going to Guze.

Once home again, we would rest for a day after which I went around carrying produce to Ma Tiny's friends who had no fields. This was followed by shelling corn and grinding it into grits for our family's consumption. If I wasn't at school, the children knew exactly where I was. If in the boat that week and the teacher called my name, they would say "in the boat" or "in the field" if that was the case. The whole class would then have a good laugh before the teacher stopped them.

On one occasion when I went to school, Tee didn't have his lunch again. A boy from Grand Turk had thrown it away and beaten him up. Well, I couldn't do anything right then during school but decided to handle that after school. This boy's class got out before my own so I missed the opportunity to straighten him out. The same afternoon, on my way home, I heard some of the bigger boys calling after me. They were saying a boy down the road was beating on Tee. I turned back to see what was going on. The boys accompanying me wanted to see if I could beat this boy, too, since I had beaten everyone who came my way. When I got there, Tee's gingerbread suit was almost off him. This boy didn't wait for any introduction. He just informed me that his plan was to give me what was left over from Tee.

I had never seen him before in my life. He was tall, slim, and dark with a few rotten teeth in his mouth. He headed toward me with bent fists.

When I thought he was close enough, I asked him, "Why did you hit Tee?"

He built his guard and threw a right at me. I moved my head back, blocked his right with my left hand, and gave him a taste of my right. Blood spilled all over the road, his clothes, and shoes. The big boys who set that fight up disappeared immediately and ran up the road. I looked at the bleeding boy and felt sorry for him, so I got some sea grape leaves for him to put over his mouth. By this time, he was crying so loudly that I thought he would die. I became afraid. When I got home, I met my stepmother ironing the clothes. I greeted her as pleasantly as I could. I felt good when she greeted me back warmly. I headed straight for the bedroom and changed out of my school clothes. Before I got back to the kitchen where Ma Tiny was, I heard someone making a noise. I stopped to listen. The boy's grandmother was telling my stepmother I was going to kill someone if they weren't careful.

Baba wasn't at home. Ma Tiny called for me after she took one look at that boy. He was standing there along with his grandmother, and his face looked disfigured.

Ma Tiny said, "Bring your little butt to me. I'm tired of telling you about fighting. I figured something was wrong when you came in with your bright 'Good afternoon.'"

She grabbed me and flogged me with that special razor-edged belt. When she was finished with me, I was burning, bleeding, itching, and hurting all over. I don't think the boy's grandmother was satisfied though, so she went up the road to Paul Grant's house, where the men were drinking. My father was there.

He asked the boy, "Who did that to you?"

His grandmother answered, "That same boy you got in your house you calling your son. He did this."

Baba came home with a tamarind switch in his left hand. He met me still scratching in one of the bedrooms. I heard him asking Ma Tiny for me.

She answered, "Mind, I already beat that boy."

But that monkey bag he was drinking told him to get me anyway. So he grabbed me with his right hand, held my two hands in his, and whipped me. I could only twist from side to side because his cuts were going into the same cuts Ma Tiny had put there earlier.

When he was finished, he told me, "That boy is your brother Othneil."

I thought, *How am I supposed to know that if no one told me?*

He had never told me, and neither had anyone else. I don't think I have forgiven my old man for that yet. He only beat me twice, this time and another time aboard the *Altiny*. The next morning after this beating, I couldn't go to school. I was in too much pain.

The beating aboard the boat took place after he saw me put my hand in one of his friend's plate. He thought I was practicing bad manners. Mr. Nickolas Missick was a passenger on the boat who became attached to me during the trip home from the Bahamas. I imagined he was missing his own children and thought of them as he played with me. The chef had prepared peas and rice mixed with pigtails and salt beef and steamed fish on the side. As I was finishing my plate, Mr. Missick told me, if I wanted more salt beef, I could take a piece out of his plate. My father saw this as he was steering. He was ashamed, thinking I didn't have manners, so he became angry. On those sailboats, a piece of rope was on both sides at the stern to help hold the tiller in place during steering. The rope was important, especially if a strong wind was blowing. He held the end of one piece of rope and hit me about five times with it. I didn't know what to do or say.

I was in so much pain that I threw up all of the food I had eaten. I ran forward, back aft, down in the cabin and still couldn't find peace of mind or place to rest. I didn't know what I had done wrong or what the beating was for. This was out of the character for my father. Mr. Missick didn't know what to do either. He became so angry at Baba that he threw his food in the sea, and he was making a fuss with him for beating me like that. He explained what took place. My father apologized to me and everyone else aboard because they were all upset with him for treating me that way. That incident taught him to ask me what happened and listen to me before making his conclusion and getting angry with me. Mr. Missick took me in his arms, and I could see his eyes fill with tears. Baba and I became friends again. The other beating brought my brother and me closer also. We were real good friends, and we used to walk to school together for the rest of his visit. Othneil and Tee ended up being good friends too.

Tee and I were always close. I liked being around him. He taught me many things I was unable to learn at home with Ma Tiny.

Everything with her was work. There was no time for playing and having fun at growing up. Tee was different. People would grab him and send him to the shop or wells or give him any other chore to do. It didn't matter whether he was on an errand for his mother. He always enjoyed the sideshow. This gave him a chance at becoming street-smart. He had many experiences of how different people lived and ran their families. People even took the risk of beating Tee if they felt it was necessary and didn't think anything of it. Sometimes he got beatings when he went home later than his mother expected him. In those days, people could whip a child if he were found doing wrong. If the parents caught wind of it, they would beat the child again because they felt the child had to have done something wrong for an adult to have to correct him.

We have allowed things to change in many cases for the worse since then, but in today's society, if an adult tried that with a child, he might find himself looking down a gun barrel. People called me proud and prejudiced because I was different from Tee. They couldn't grab me and beat me like that. I would hit them back. I had to be home all the time, but he could go out. My father never stayed home to teach me anything on becoming a man. I had no big brother or uncle to tell me what's what. It was always Ma Tiny. When I wasn't washing, I was cooking or ironing. I hated ironing. I supposed washing was okay until I had to wash Ma Tiny's clothes.

One incident happened while I was ironing one day. We used a goose iron then and filled it with coal, lit it, allowed it to heat up, cleaned it properly, and then began to iron. Ma Tiny put some clothes in the chair and fixed a pad on the table. We had no ironing board back then. We used the table. I was ready even though I didn't feel like ironing. I looked over the clothes in the chair and saw one of her good outfits. I brought that old goose inside and ironed about three pieces. I decided it needed heating up so I put it outside in the wind. When I brought it inside, it was red-hot. So I took that nice outfit and began to iron it. I rested the iron in one spot too long. When I moved the iron, there was a hole in the outfit, the shape of the iron. And there, stuck to the bottom of the iron, was the missing piece.

Ma Tiny came running into the room just then, inquiring about the burning smell. She saw the burnt dress and me holding the iron in my hand. I knew what was going to happen. She took the iron out of my hand and pushed me aside. I fell to the floor. She held up the outfit, looked at it again, and went for her special belt, inviting me in her usual hostile manner to come to her so she could teach me some sense. She informed me, "You are stupid, an idiot; and a fool." She told me "Your father would be better off carrying you in the boat to help him work." She beat me until she was tired. She was breathing hard. She never gave me clothes to press again. Secretly, I rejoiced. I thought I won that one. But I still had several other chores I had to do continuously.

On holidays, Christmas, and other occasions, my stepmother would go to whatever function and leave me home to work. Sometimes, according to where it was happening, I could hear my friends enjoying themselves. A popular activity used to be playing the maypole. A tall pole was planted with colored strings attached, usually in even numbers. The same numbers of persons each took a string and danced around to the beat of a rip-saw band.[2] Holding these strings, people danced in and out until the strings were plaited. Then everyone

---

2   The rip-saw band was made up of simple instruments, mostly tools and homemade appliances. There was an accordion, a handsaw, a knife, and a goatskin drum. A goat was killed, and the hide was used to construct the drum. (Sometimes the hide was brought in from Haiti.) All the hair was removed. It was stretched over the box and attached with small tacks. Before being used, it was heated over a fire.

danced in the opposite direction to unplait the strings. The person who got his string loose first was the winner.

During dance exercises, the girls helped to make music sweeter. As they wound their bodies like caterpillars, they looked over their shoulders at their male partners as to say, "Don't touch me!" The guys danced behind the ladies, winding like snakes with one hand on the belly and the other behind the neck as they answered the ladies refrain, "I coming!" While all the fun went on, the men drank claren, the women drank cherry brandy, and the children had Haitian cola. I was home drinking water and working. Whenever I got back to school, the children mocked me.

Every once in a while, I would sneak a peek to see what was going on and imagine myself dancing the maypole while I watched the crowd. Then I would hurry home before Ma Tiny sent someone to check on me to find out whether I was sleeping or working.

I started working very early in my life. My mother once asked my stepmother to let me go to East Harbor with her. I had to leave school for one month. My brother Mackie liked getting in the tub when it was time to bathe. This time, he got into the tub before the water was there. There was only one lamp so the kitchen was dark. Aunt Tit, my mother's last sister, was preparing for the bath. She knew where the tub was but didn't know that Mackie was already inside of it. She got the pot of hot water and poured the hot water in the tub. At that point, Mackie screamed. He was scalded all over his chest. You could imagine how he looked. I thought my brother would die.

No doctor was in Blue Hills. The nearest one was in South Caicos, so he had to endure that pain for four days until he could get to the doctor. There were no speedboats or planes to transport him, but my grandmother Jane Palmer and aunt-in-law Estella Parker were the best bush doctors around. I assumed that they were the best in the entire country. They looked after Mackie with their homemade remedies until Mr. Archie Capron's boat, the SS *Lady Sheriff*, was ready to sail to East Harbor. The trip lasted for one and a half days. After Mackie saw the doctor a couple times, I began to feel good because I could see he was getting better.

I got a job to haul bonefish with Mr. Gue Jennings and sell them to help Mommy take care of us, especially Mackie. Gue Jennings was my stepmother's nephew. I had gotten to know him earlier when I stayed in East Harbor with my stepmother while she was looking after his mother during her illness. After about a month, Mackie was running lively again.

You wouldn't believe how important it was to be able to fight. In those days, most of the children from Grand Turk, South Caicos, and Salt Cay thought or acted as if they were superior to the children from the Caicos Islands. They referred to us as the "Corkas" people. Sometimes they even referred to us as "west-of-the-buoy people," and we referred to them as "salt rakers." So I had to fight better to deal with that. As I got older though, I never had a problem with any of them. I always had many friends. Everyone knew Charlie Palmer.

I had a few narrow escapes in my life that I didn't forget easily. At the age of twelve, I went with my stepfather to fetch his boat. High winds forced him to leave Boma Road earlier that week. When he came home from the Bahamas, he wanted a boat even though he wasn't a fisherman. He didn't have the money, but his loving mother forgave him for wasting all those years in the Bahamas and gave him the money to begin building his dinghy.

In a few months, the boat was finished, and he thought he was ready for a life as a boatman. One day, he took his mother and his wife down Boma Road to cut sisal, but the wind blew so hard that he had to leave the boat there and walk back home. Days later, the wind fell for a few hours in the morning so he felt it was safe to bring it home. He asked my mother if I could go with him. They were together, husband and wife, so she didn't want to deny him the privilege of being with her children, so she allowed me to go. We called him "Uncle Uriel" like the other children who were his nieces and nephews.

He had already sought pardon for leaving her all these years soon after they were married. He accepted us as his stepchildren and never made my mother feel inferior about having us with another man because it was entirely his fault that she did. On the other hand, he was absolutely disrespectful to his mother and used to curse her to the lowest. She always told him he would die an untimely death because of his dishonorable attitude toward her.

We set out walking down the beach where the boat was. On our way, we heard that my sick uncle was dying. He had now been sick for a long period. In fact, his casket was already made.[3] We got to the boat, just my stepfather and me, and put it in the water. We filled a few sacks of sand for ballast and started our journey. He took his fishing line with him because he wanted to catch a barracuda to take back with him.

We jumped in the boat and headed for the reef. By this time, the wind was strong, the sea was getting rough, and the current was pulling strong. I became afraid and pleaded with him to turn back to shore. I said, "Uncle Uriel, please turn back, let's go to the shore and we could track the boat up." He said, "No, I have to get a barracuda, I really have to get one." He kept on explaining, "I have to go out further if I am going to catch one. We will be okay." As we continued to head for the reef, we almost sank. I decided right there and then that he couldn't handle the boat. Before he had left these islands, he had worked with his family, who were small-scale farmers, and he

---

3   At that time, there was no way of preserving the dead, so they had to be buried the same day. Because of that, it was the regular custom to build one's casket if one got sick unto death.

was hardly able to master that, so being a boatman was a little to the extreme.

Growing up with my father and being around boats all the time, I had an idea, but I was only twelve years old so I could only do as he said. We got almost to the reef and tacked back. We made it to the shore safely. Onshore, I pleaded with him to track the boat along the shore, only to have him tell me to stop talking bologna. At this time, he tacked back and headed for the reef again. This time, the wind seemed to be blowing harder. We almost sank again. I suggested we take short tacks as I didn't want to tell him right out that he didn't know what he was doing. I became afraid.

I kept telling myself, "If he stays close to the shore, I would feel so much better."

But it was no use. We continued on our course to the reef. All of a sudden, the barracuda he wanted to catch so badly appeared to be on the line. He wanted to handle the line with the barracuda on it and the tiller at the same time, so he instructed me to tack back. He failed to give me enough time to shift the ballast as he always did when we were tacking. Shifting the ballast helped the boat to stand up better rather than trimming the jib. Trying to hold on to the line and handle the tiller was his mistake. Instantly, the boat cut right under the water straight to the bottom. This water was about twenty feet deep.

When I caught myself, I looked aft, but he wasn't there. Then I saw him in the water.

I asked, "What are we going to do?"

He said, "We'll have to take the mast out of the boat."

So I dove down and tried to find the knife to cut the rope, but I couldn't. I tried to untie the rope but couldn't do that either. With the water being about twenty feet deep and the boat on the seabed, I couldn't stay down long. Each time I went down and reached the boat, I was nearly out of breath. The sea was rough with the wind blowing hard. I couldn't even see land. My heart was pounding. I realized we were in big trouble.

I mustered up my courage. "We must swim to the shore."

He replied, "Let's go off the wind because it would be easier."

He was pointing toward the Wheeland Cut, and I remembered my father telling me how strong the current pulled in that cut.

So I said to him, "No, I'm going this way." At twelve years old, my mind was leading me to head for the houses I could barely see in the distance.

He agreed with me. "We'll meet on shore."

I started swimming but looked back. I saw him trying to grab me.

"Can you swim?" I asked.

He didn't say, but I didn't let him catch on to me or my clothes. I thought that would be dangerous or even fatal. I went under the angry water and swam away. When I came up for air and checked on him, I only saw his cap floating on the water. I figured he was swimming under the water, too, trying to keep up with me, so I continued to swim toward the land. When I looked the second time and still only saw his cap, I began to feel scared. Thinking now that something must have happened to him, I tried to keep myself from panicking and having negative thoughts. I pondered the thought that I might be alone and with yet a long distance to swim. I swam until my arms were tired. The waves were breaking in my face. I could hardly see as I drank saltwater every now and then. I decided I should turn on my back for a while and rest my arms. To my surprise, I was nearly back where I started.

I began to swim again, this time from side to side, trying to keep up my strength. I was very tired and frequently floated for a while to regain a little strength. Soon, I felt something under my feet. I was startled and jumped out of fear, thinking it was a shark. To my amazement and relief, it was a coral head. Realizing this, I stood on it and rested for a while. Uncle Uriel, my stepfather, was nowhere in sight. I considered my distance to shore and figured I was halfway. I felt new courage to go on. When I started swimming again, I thought about Uncle Uriel and wondered if he were almost ashore.

When I got tired again, I had the same amazing thing happen. Another coral head was under my feet! Was this a miracle from God? I feel now it was. This time, I wasn't too frightened. As I stood up, I could see the beach clearly and knew I was almost on land. I didn't rest very long because I wanted to finish this unpleasant journey. This time, I swam until my feet touched the ground. I was happy to be on land again. As I felt triumph in my heart that I was safe, panic struck me when, all of a sudden, I heard a sound behind me. It sounded as if the water opened, turned around, and went back out. I felt more frightened at this than during the whole ordeal. I looked around and saw nothing, only the water moving in its rage. I walked up high enough on the sand to see if Uncle Uriel's footprints were in the sand, but there were none. I was tired. Every muscle and limb hurt. I took a nap, knowing Uncle Uriel would have to pass that way and he could wake me up. I lay crosswise on the beach so he could see me.

I dozed off quickly. I don't know how long I slept.

A voice awakened me. "Are you dead?"

I wondered it myself. *Am I dead?* I thought he was telling me I was dead. This was my friend riding a horse; I recognized his voice, heard the horse make a familiar sound and opened my eyes. That's when I knew I was still alive. He told me, "We were watching the boat and were wondering why you all did not turn back." "Why didn't you all bring the boat to shore and track it up?" I replied, "Uncle Uriel would just not do it; I told him that over and over." "Well," he said, "I was not worried about you; I know that you can swim." We often swam together, rode horses together, and dived for conchs together. We used to take his dad's dinghy and come back with a load of conchs for his father to take out of the shells because we didn't know how. We dove with our naked eyes, meaning no masks.

I returned to reality. Uncle Uriel and I had left home early that morning to get the boat, around seven o'clock. We were coming right back so I didn't eat breakfast. I reckon I swam about two and a half hours, and now it was after eleven. I jumped on the horse with my friend, telling him the sad story as we rode to my Uncle Eric's house in Corinize. When we arrived at his house, only the small children were home. All the adults had gone to my sick uncle Salathiel's house where he lay dying, or so they thought. My friend left me there and went to tell my parents what I had told him. I didn't have any food because there was no one to fix it. So I walked over to my uncle's house, where everyone were standing and waiting around to witness his passing.

I tried telling my story to some of them, but no one took me seriously. So I went toward home by way of the beach, where I found a crowd of curious people wanting to hear an account of what took place. My friend had already alerted them, and they wanted to know exactly what happened.

My father was glad to see me. "Go home, eat breakfast, change into dry clothes, and then come back to the beach to tell your tale."

I returned, and after I told them my story, the men planned their strategy for the search. Some of the men had five horse power engines attached to their dinghies. They went in the direction where I told them we were and where they last saw the boat before it sunk.

They looked all over the area, found the boat, got it afloat, and brought it home. But they never found him. Some people walked along the beach in case he had swam in and was lying on the beach waiting to be rescued. Other persons rode horses so, if he were found, he could be brought back without an exertion on his part. They took a thermos with hot tea and a bowl of soup to nourish him, but their search was futile. This went on for several days until it was concluded to the people's satisfaction that he had drowned. I feared that boat until it came to the end of its usefulness. The boat was sold several weeks after the incident. Even though the new owners worked it and never died or came to any harm, I was sure I didn't want anything to do with that dinghy.

Another close call occurred one night when I was sleeping at my grandmother Jane Palmer's. Her house was in the same yard as my father's, and I used to sleep over there, especially when my parents went out. This night, they were out. My grandmother decided to go out after I fell asleep. She was an inquisitive person, always trying to get involved in other people's affairs, especially when she was drinking. So after putting me to bed, she sneaked out to take a drink. Someone who wanted to get even saw her leaving and decided to take this opportunity to do so. Her house was wooden with a thatched roof and didn't need kerosene or gasoline to start a fire. A little spark could easily put that dry thatch to flame, and that's exactly what that person did … with me inside. I was sleeping peacefully and ignorant of the house burning around me.

After the word got out that Ma Jane's house was on fire, the crowd grew quickly. My parents barely got me out in time before the side I was sleeping on fell in. They didn't remember I was in there at first. Was this another miracle?

Chapter Two

First Job, First Love, Bad Friends (1960s)

After leaving school at the tender age of thirteen, I went straight to work on the boat with my dad. He finally listened to my stepmother and took me out of school. In those days, people bullied lobster.[4] We were always the last dinghy to come back to the vessel in the evenings. While those other boats were bringing in six and eight hundred lobsters, Baba would have like two hundred. I was just starting out and wasn't sure what I could do. I felt I could do better if I were in the bow.

In spite of this, I had plenty of fun being with the big boys, making my own money, even though I never saw a penny of it. I still felt like I was man among men. The only thing I didn't like about going in the boat was the times when we had to walk to Five Cays from North Side. During the winter months, the weather would get rough on the north side so the boats couldn't get out of the cut. On the southern side though, the weather would be good enough to go out to French Cay area so the boatmen would leave the boats in Five Cays. When the boats were left in Five Cays, we would have to walk through the land.

This trip would usually begin at one in the morning. Walking barefoot over rocks in the dark, carrying heavy loads on our heads,

---

4   A bully was a contraption made of a fifteen-foot staff, a piece of rebar steel, and some netting that was attached by using a few sixpenny nails. A peg was used to help ease the lobster out from the shoal far enough to be trapped and caught. This peg was attached to a staff that was just as long as the bully staff.

with another small package in hand was our custom. My responsibility was to carry a fifty-pound bag of flour on my head and a change of clothes in my hand. In the dark, we traveled the narrow road mainly by guessing and instinct. Over hills and down valleys, we would go, stopping only twice or so before the seven-mile journey ended. By then, I would have acquired three busted toes and prickles or sticks from dry branches in my tired, aching feet. I was sure my feet were hard enough to walk over broken bottles without being cut.

The dinghies at Five Cays beach would take us to the anchored vessels. When we got underway, we would proceed to West Caicos and work for the day. In the evening, we would pick firewood and get water. If we were heading down the bank, we could get water at the fresh well on Long Bay beach in the morning and still reach across the bank in time to work most of the day. We used to fill up canoes with lobster and wait for the pickup boat. The *Mary Rose* came twice a week from Mike Burris's fish plant and collected from all the boats. If for some reason the pickup boat couldn't come out to us, then we would go into South Caicos to take our catch.

On the second trip of the week, the pickup boat brought the money for the first set of fish. By the weekend, if the north side was still rough, we went back to Five Cays to secure the boats. This would go on until the weather permitted us to go on the north side. I had corns on my hands from sculling. That's hard work. I was glad when my father bought a five horse power engine about two months later. It was great, easier on my hands, and got me where I wanted to go much faster. I still had to keep up at the coral head, where the bowman was bullying lobster. In the stern of the boat, I would have to pay close attention so I would know when to threw the peg to the bowman and catch it when he threw it back.

When he threw it back, I knew he was ready to bring a lobster in the boat. This exercise was carried out all day and every day, except Saturday and Sunday. On Saturday, we would clean our boats and rest. On Sunday, we would attend church. I enjoyed the journeys to South Caicos most. We would sell our catch, get paid, buy our supplies, collect some salt, and come home. We were usually home in time for church, but I preferred to go to Sunday school in the afternoon so I could show off my new clothes and felt hat. We were paid in pounds, shillings, and pence. Lobster was going for a penny a pound and was plentiful then. We thought it would always be that way. There was so much lobster to be had that a song was made up about it.

Laugh, girl, laugh. Laugh, girl, laugh. Laugh, girl, laugh. Come, we got lobster money!

Lobster money never done. Lobster money. Lobster money is a lot of fun. Lobster money!

Lobster was everywhere. A fisherman could work one rock all day. You could move the smaller lobsters aside and reach for the bigger ones. They were often stacked one on top of each other. Scale fish were plentiful then too. You could catch a big muttonfish or grouper with bare hands. These fish were in competition with the fisherman for lobster. Sometimes they tried, literally, to take them from the fishermen. The seafood was plentiful, and the money was small, but we made it. By that time, Baba would give me enough money to buy clothes and shoes, if I could find any to fit. You see, my feet are big so I wear size thirteen. So as a teen, my feet were much bigger than the average boy my age. Because of this, it was difficult to find the correct size for me.

I became friends with one of the crewmembers, George Cunningham. He and his cousin Perry worked together on my father's boat. George and I became best friends. In fact, he was like an older brother. We even dressed alike back then. Harold and Betty Krent built another fish plant, the Shell Factory, on South Caicos in the Conch Ground area. They bought lobster and conch shells. They also opened a variety store that had nearly everything worthwhile in it. This couple had their own boat as well, the MV *Shell Factory*, so they kept up with the latest in fashions and new inventions. George and I became very popular among the girls in South Caicos, but three girls working at the Shell Factory, Dora Lightbourne and Mavis and Kathleen Harvey, became our special friends. We were more like brothers and sisters. They knew we wanted to be the two best-dressed guys, so they would pick out our outfits and save them for us until we went back to South Caicos. If we didn't go one week, they would keep them there knowing we would pay for them.

Back in Providenciales on Sunday afternoon, we would dress and go up the road to the church where Sunday school was being held. We knew most of the girls would be there, so we would use Hair Glo to condition our hair and make it shine and used our "cush cush" cologne. At the church, we used the door that the wind was blowing through to make our grand entrance. Everyone would smell our fragrance, and we could hear their whispers, "That's George and Charlie." They didn't have to turn their heads, but did anyway. We knew not many smelled like us. We used to light up the church with a wonderful aroma. As we walked in, all of the girls would be making space beside them for us to sit.

The days were getting better, but I was still not satisfied with the catch in our dinghy. The other boats were still getting more lobster than we did, so I asked Baba one day to let me try bullying, but he said I was too young. Well, I stayed in the stern that day, and after everyone finished for the day, my friend Herman Grant and I took the boat and went to learn to bully. Since we were the same age and companions, we wanted to challenge each other. He was in the same predicament as I was because his older brother Patrick Grant (Gawland) wouldn't allow him to go in the bow either because of his youth.

When we got to the shoal, I allowed him to try first because he was smaller than I was. He gave up quickly, and I took my turn. As I looked into the water glass, I saw numerous lobsters and began to try to bully them. Just before dark, we went back to the sloop. The men were amazed at how much lobster we caught. My father was surprised. We got more lobster within that short time than he and I had gotten all day. He was proud of me.

The next morning when we went off, my father took the stern of the dinghy. I didn't think he was giving up his position as the bowman, but that's what he was doing. As we got to the shoal, he turned off the engine and took up the oar. I still didn't move.

He said to me, "What are you waiting for? Check for lobster in the rock and start bullying."

I knew then that I was the bowman, but now I had to get used to all that bending all day. By the end of the first day, my back was killing me. My system soon got used to it though because I was accustomed to hard work. Pretty soon, our dinghy ranked second on the *Wheeland Queen*.

Shortly after this incident, the method of accumulating lobster changed. People began to dive and toss. The men in South Caicos started first, and then they showed Marshall Ewing, a Haitian national, how to make the toss. The teachers were the Cox brothers from South Caicos, who were originally from Blue Hills. They learned to do it in Miami from some Cuban American who was happy to show them how to make it and use it. They were the first in the country to use the toss, and they were the best for a short while until the Blue Hills boys learned how to use it. Marshall showed George who, in turn, taught me how to make and use the toss. It consisted of a noose attached to a four-foot staff three quarters of an inch in circumference. We would use two staplers to hold the wire on the staff and two spindles for the wire to slip through up and down on the next side. We would dive and try to get it over the lobster tail at the same time.

At first, we didn't have the hang of it and cut more lobster than we caught. But after a while, we had it under control. We had to learn the art of it. Soon, Marshall was one of the best on the bank, and I later moved to one of the best as well. He was the leading man on board the *Sea Fan*, and I was the boss on the *Wheeland Queen*. With me in my father's dinghy bow, the guys gained respect for Baba. They were unable to laugh at his catch anymore because it was now big as theirs or bigger. I became one of the best lobster divers in Turks and Caicos and one of the few divers who could go to the deepest depth until the doctors stopped me. Fifty feet was my daily dive routine without any flippers. They came later on in the development of lobster diving.

I also enjoyed making rope. Mr. Livingstone Swann used to travel to the Bahamas from Turks and Caicos. He used to bring back pieces of large rope he got from other bigger boats he met during his travel. He would share this with all the owners of boats so they would have rope too. These ropes were very thick so we divided the strands and remade rope in the size we needed. These open strands were tied and piled up until Saturday afternoon when most of the men were free to come and give a hand during the making of the rope.

After leaving school, I enjoyed my boat life, especially when going to the Big South. Those weeks we knew we would be going, we worked extra hard, anticipating the excitement of spending the night in the Big South. While I was old enough to make money, I wasn't old enough to spend it or have any control over it, as the custom went. In fact, the men back then only wanted to have their sons do the work, but they, the fathers, controlled their money. I was too young to go to the bars and hops (disco) so my father often left me aboard the boat. Sometimes though, the boys sneaked me ashore. They always got me back before my father returned. The hot spots in East Harbor were Mr. Lloyd Stubbs's, Hugh Wilson's, and Oswald Jennings's places. Oswald was my stepmother's nephew.

We usually anchored at Conch Ground after we sold our catch and bought supplies for the next week or so. We boys liked to work the bank toward South Caicos so we could spend Friday and Saturday evenings there. That place used to come alive on those nights. Many times, all I could do was sit inside the cabin door and listen to Tom T. Hall and Hank Williams singing country music from a distance. The hot spots played other Caribbean and Jamaican music too. The sounds drifted in simultaneously as I sat in the cabin door, deciding whom to listen to. I would still be sitting there when everyone returned to the boat, just listening as the wind brought the lovely sound over the air or until those places closed down.

That's how it went forever, or so it seemed. But one Thursday afternoon, I got my chance. We were on our way sailing from Man-O-War Bush toward Six Hill Cay to anchor for the night. My father told George that he, Perry, and I would take two dinghies and carry the lobster into South Caicos to sell. We were to wait until moonrise before we tried to go back to the boat. At first, I didn't want to go because Baba told George to take me to Mrs. Helene Jennings, Oswald Jennings's wife, until it was time to come back to the boat. George went under deck and put together the clothes that he would carry. I wasn't interested in going. I had a problem with my parents' logic. They thought I was old enough to work and be one of the best divers on the bank, but not old enough to go ashore and be among the boys I worked with. I protested strongly, but George coaxed me to go with them. I didn't know what plan he had, but I went anyway.

George and I were in the boat in front with the small engine pulling the next boat with Perry in it. We talked the whole way to

South Caicos with the water gushing all over us when the waves broke. When we reached the fisheries, we met an old friend, Mr. Alexander Thomas. He befriended all the Caicos fishermen. He was waiting to count our catch. When we finished, George inquired about water and told me to shower first. I didn't see any point since I didn't have any clothes to change into. He continued to hurry me up, so I did. To my surprise, he had clean clothes for me. I couldn't believe my eyes or ears. Then he told me, while my father was giving the instructions, he was below deck getting my clothes out of Baba's suitcase. I was very happy he did.

We went on to Mrs. Helene to say hello and then all over the place to find friends. They asked us what we had planned and invited us to go along with them. We told them we were only staying for a few hours. At the Wilson's Club, we saw one of our lady friends who was giving a farewell party, and she invited us to stay. She was leaving on the *Shell Factory* for Miami the next day. I know I was a little young, but I stood tall and had a little mustache, so I looked seventeen or eighteen years old. We joined the party, and George gave me a St. Pauli Girl beer and then another one. I began to feel good. We danced, we ate, and I had one more beer. It was soon time to say good-bye. We shook hands and left, heading back to the boat. From Six Hill Cay, we could see a light in the distance. We knew it was the *Wheeland Queen*, and it steered us back to where the boat was. We had already changed into our old boat clothes when we got on board. My father, thinking I had napped some at Mrs. Helene's, encouraged us to take another short nap before time to start work again.

They told me, as soon as I started to sleep, I started singing the "Russian Satellite." The Mighty Sparrow sang it. They played this song at the party, and I fell in love with it, so I sang it even in my sleep. My father suspected something and asked, "Charlie, were you at the club last night?" "No sir," I replied. "I heard that song at Mrs. Helene's place." While he questioned me, George took that time to put my clothes back in his suitcase. To ease his suspicion, my father went to check my clothes but found them neatly folded, just like they were before.

The next day, we were happy and energetic. We filled all of the canoes in a couple of hours. We were ready to go back to South Caicos and have more fun. We were in South Caicos that Friday afternoon, had sold our catch and cleaned our boats, and were ready to go ashore. My old man didn't mind me going with George this time, but he insisted that I not stay too long. He made it clear I couldn't stay all night. We enjoyed ourselves and headed back to the boat about ten thirty. Early the next morning, we did our necessary chores in preparation for our return voyage to Blue Hills.

In 1956, Mr. G. O. Lightbourne and Mrs. Oseta Jolly decided it was time to start looking into building better roads in Blue Hills. Mr. Lightbourne was the elected representative; Mrs. Jolly was the head mistress of the Blue Hills primary school. The first phase of the road was built in the area of the school where other government property was located. The schoolteacher's residence, a guesthouse for government visiting dignitaries, and a public water cistern were located there. There was also a jetty for the boats used to ferry officials.

The road began from the end of the jetty, into the building area, and then down past the Browns' and up past the Ewings'. The road was made of cracked stones mixed with damp mud. Most of the stones used were taken from old walls that had been used to fence individual properties. The mud came from the pond that ran almost all through the settlement of Blue Hills. I suppose people were willing to sell those rocks for little or nothing to secure better roads. Workers moved rocks and mud by carrying away loads on their heads. The skilled men were paid five shillings per day, and laborers received two shillings. Still, everybody was happy to have better roads.

The first bicycle I had in Blue Hills was a Hercules, British made. The road was about a half mile up and down then. About three bikes were on the island before mine, but they were fixed wheels.[5] Mr. Hilly Ewing, Hearts Capron, and Llewellyn Ewing owned three of these bikes, and they often rode them up on the hill to the beginning of the jetty. They had many hours of fun riding those bikes. I enjoyed watching them. I told my father I would like to have one. He didn't answer me, but three weeks later, he made a trip to Grand Turk. When he was leaving from Grand Turk, he sent an announcement over the cable and wireless radio that I should meet the boat in Five Cays that afternoon.

I left home about noon that day. To me, it was scary for one person to walk to Five Cays from Blue Hills because people told stories that were wicked, about hearing sounds of babies crying when you reach Pasture Well. Some of these people believed in witchcraft and made these stories sound real. I walked to Five Cays alone that day and didn't see or hear anything out of the ordinary. I got in to Five Cays and went straight to the beach. I saw the *Wheeland Queen* just in and anchored, and the crew was tying up the sails. During this time, the North Side was rough so the boat was taken in to Five Cays. The men got in the dinghy in preparation to come ashore. As they got closer, I could see a bicycle in the dinghy. I felt sure it was mine. My heart swelled with pride, even though I didn't know for sure that it was mine.

---

5   A fixed wheel has no brakes. They had to be stopped by using the pedals. So if you tried to speed during a ride and stopped suddenly, the bike would throw you over the handlebar so fast that you would think you were riding a cow.

My father jumped out of the boat and rubbed my head. "Is everything all right?" Then he confirmed my suspicion. "That's your bike."

I thanked my father, wrapped him tight, laughed, and then took the bike to check it out. That bike had everything: headlamp, taillight, mirror on each handlebar, siren, bell, ribbons in the handlebars, brakes, black towing racks, fenders, and reflectors. I had never seen a bike with everything before. I even had spare tires. Preston Malcolm really fixed my bike for me. He used to work for Timco Ltd. at that time.

Baba asked, "Do you want to wait for some of the men who were walking to Blue Hills?"

But I couldn't wait to get my beautiful bike home. It was really a beauty, green with white trimmings. "I'll begin alone because I want to show it off."

All of the men weren't coming to North Side. Some were staying on board to look after the cargo and bring the boat round when the weather was suitable.

The road between the settlements was rough in some places, so I had to carry the bike most of the way. Most of the other children who saw me looked on in awe. Some said, "You can't speak to him now." I was proud of my bike. At home, I cleaned it up and went back out riding. After having my bike for some weeks, more bikes were coming to the island, but I was still a star.

One day, I parked it down the road and walked up to the schoolyard to take a break. No vehicles were on the island so we had the road to ourselves. The boys began to race, but I wasn't interested. I was still resting. One boy who didn't have a bike took mine without asking and joined the race. When I saw what he was doing and began calling out to him, he couldn't hear. He was gone. Suddenly, I saw one of the boys fall down, and I hoped it wasn't my bike. All the other boys came back, and as they approached, I realized my bike was on the ground back there. The boy who stole my bike ran toward the beach and all the way home so I couldn't get near him.

My bike was in a mess. The front wheel was badly bent, so bad that it couldn't roll. The back wheel was twisted; the light and bell were broken. I looked at the bike again and looked at the other boys who, by this time, had come back. I was trying to decide what to do. Someone suggested I go to his parents so I took the broken bike, put it on my head, and headed to his parents. As I approached the hill on which they lived, the father came out to meet me. I suppose they were expecting me since this boy had run home. "If you come any closer, you bush-born bastard, I will throw you off of my property. Get out of my yard now." His father-in-law heard him and came out to see what the matter was. When I told him the story, he was hurt about the way his son-in-law handled the situation.

He told him, "That boy is going to be a man one day; I hope you will remember that. I do not like how you are bringing up your children, that is the wrong way." He told me, "Charlie, you go home and tell your parents what happened." The thing that bothered me was that this man called himself my father's best friend. They were so close that my father kept a bottle of Beefeater Gin at the head of his bed for this man to have a drink when he visited his house. At our house, this family was the "big mockety mock." They ate and drank only the best when they were visiting. I couldn't go in the room they were occupying during their visits. On occasions when he was visiting alone, if he got drunk after drinking too much gin, he became frightened, and I had to walk him to his house. Our house was near Bethany Baptist Church, and the cemetery was nearby. About a half mile further down, there are two other cemeteries. So I had the job of walking him because my father was scared also. Sometimes I only walked him past the graveyard before I turned back.

I went home just like the old man told me to and spoke to my parents. When my father told him about the way he handled me, he said his son told him I had loaned him the bicycle, and he didn't steal it. He also informed my father that I was a liar. My father didn't make a fuss and sent to Grand Turk for new wheels, fender, lights, and everything needed to repair it. I fixed my bike, and Baba got a lock for me this time. After that, every time I jumped off it, I locked it up. That way, no one could move it unless I gave him permission.

Work on building the road stopped and started for short periods. Mr. G. O. Lightbourne was still the representative for the people so he was seeking ways to help. Because all the government offices were in Grand Turk, the payroll took too long, and money ran out before it got down to the working people. There was an inquiry into who would be able to pay the workers when the weekend came around because a check from Grand Turk would be slow getting there. A few persons tried covering the wages, but they thought the reimbursement was still not fast enough. Finally, Mr. Harry Ewing, the district constable, and my father decided they would do it. Mr. Ewing paid the people who lived and worked south of the school, and my father took care of the people north of the school. Under these two men, the road was completed to the two ends of the Blue Hills settlement.

Things began to change for the better in 1966 when Mr. Fritz Luddington, an enterprising American investor, came to Blue Hills. An administrator, Mr. Golding, was leading the government of the Turks and Caicos Islands. He served as administrator from 1965 to 1967. Gus Lightbourne was still serving as the people's representative in the legislative assembly. We were not at the level of government that we are now. The administrator was the representative to the British government. In the early 1960s, the only hotel in Turks and Caicos was the Admiral's Arms, located in South Caicos. Liam Maguire owned it. There were no other hotels that we even heard about.

The government bought the Turks Head Inn for tourists or investors to stay at while visiting Grand Turk. Maguire had already had Esso gas coming to South Caicos and in Leeward Going Through by the time Mr. Luddington came, so he built a small airstrip for private planes to land on in Blue Hills. When Mr. Luddington first made his visit, he came on his boat, the *Seven Dwarfs*, but later he came in a single-engine seaplane. After he decided he wanted to invest in Providenciales, my first job for Mr. Luddington was to carry his water jug from place to place for him. I never remember more rambling all over the place as when we were looking for the best areas to build. One day, a barge came in with a bulldozer, grader, roller, dump truck, pickup truck, and a Hillman car for Mr. Luddington. These were the first pieces of equipment in Providenciales in 1966. The barge came in to Long Point in the Bight. We were there early that morning to witness its arrival.

Most of the people on the island had never seen such a sight, except for those who traveled to the Bahamas or other countries, so this was an exciting day. We stood and watched in amazement as the barge came right onto the shore and dropped its ramp on the beach. The first piece of equipment to come off was the bulldozer. The only operator on the island, Mr. Bill Dudson, who came here to work for Mr. Luddington, got onto the bulldozer, started it, and began to move it. At the gurgling sound and awkward movements, we started laughing. Nearly everyone was there, including the teachers and students. The students were allowed to come and watch this unique chapter in history unravel, and we were informed that many lessons would be learned from this experience.

Billy Duson told me to help keep the children out of the way. I wasn't sure whether I was hired or not yet but was proud to be giving orders. He then dropped the dozer blade and started pushing a road from the brink of the sandbank over onto firm land. He back-bladed the track and then took the grader to smooth it off. Next, the roller came off and then the trucks. They were on their way to building roads in our island home in no time. I didn't get hired that day. Nor did I get hired for a long while. I went there every day looking for employment but got the same reply each time. I wondered, *Am I unlucky?*

One morning, I went up to the pond about six thirty where they were working and started watching this native boy dredge. I looked at every action he took, trying to figure out how to operate that machine. I stayed there until he went for lunch. He left the engine running, so I jumped on and began to operate it. The other workers stopped what they were doing and stared at me, but that didn't take away my courage. I continued to dredge and did so for a half hour. At twelve thirty, I saw a white man and the native operator coming, so I stopped and jumped off. I started to leave, but the white fellow called me back and asked, "Who told you to use the machine?" I answered honestly and told him that "I had permission from no one." He then questioned the hired man about the extent of the work he had gotten done all morning and wanted to know who did the rest. He inquired: "Who did all of this work?" The hired man said, "It must be him," referring to me. He compared the amount of work done by both of us in five and a half hours, asked, "What is your name young man?" I said "Charles Palmer." He then advised, "You are hired." He sent the original operator back to the machine shop and kept me on the dredger. I was paid for that whole day. I worked between the machine shop and the dredger. I watched everyone as they worked and became good at fixing the engines as well. The generator that provided power for the inns and staff quarters was in the shop. It was like I got good at everything I touched. Later, I worked on the roller and then the bulldozer, but didn't work on the grader.

Then trouble started. One day, we were working in Long Bay Hills. I was late picking up my payroll. Our family friend, my best friend's father, said he would get it for me. He not only received it, he opened it and discovered I was making more than his son was. He couldn't believe his eyes. I had thirteen pounds five shillings and his son had twelve pounds two shillings.[6] The father's pay was ten pounds. He operated the cement mixer.

He stormed back into the office and demanded this mistake be corrected because there was no way Charlie Palmer could be making more money than his son who was an operator. This incident began a long line of problems on the job. The heads of departments were getting at each other's throats because of it. If I drove the company truck home, it was the same story. This man became a nuisance on the job. His attitude was that his son was above me. He asked that his son be the one to drive the truck home, drop off the employees, and park it in his yard each evening.

Realizing there was no future there for me, that is, no peace or quiet, I quit the job the next year and went to the Bahamas for a while. The trip to the Bahamas was the first long flight I took. That plane barked the whole way to Nassau. I had an earache the whole night and next day.

We stopped in Nassau for one day and then went to Freeport. I traveled with my brother-in-law and stayed with my aunt in Freeport. It was a nice change from the boat life, but at times, I missed home and wished I were back. Things were different from what I was used to. I wasn't as free as I should or ought to have been. The house was a five-room, including the bath. Three boys were sharing two twin beds. I had had to share a bed with the thinnest boy. It was better when I made my bed on the floor. Back home, since the age of fifteen, I had my own room, so I had to make major adjustments to cope. Using this twin bed, I often found myself on the floor. Sometimes I felt I got pushed intentionally.

---

6   Those were the days when we used pounds, shillings, and pence.

A fishing boat that I bought for my father

Bartending at Third Turtle Inn 1976

Me in happier times

Met with Ambassador Andrew Young in Atlanta 2001

My daughter Pamela and her family

My beautiful wife Zenneth

My daughter Lacal

My daughter Sabrina and her family

My daughter Vanessa and her son Dustin

My extended family

My mother Emily

My father Thomas after winning a race at South Caicos Regatta in 1970 with Lym McGuire looking on

My father-in-law Livingston Swann

My mother-in-law Christiana Swann

My son Wayne and his family

My stepmother Altiny and I

My team just after winning a golf tournament game

My wife and grandchildren in 2007

My wife and I having a cocktail

Seeing a tourist friend off at the airport in 1976

The house I grew up in

The tombs where my father, stepmother, and grandmother were laid to rest

Chapter Three

First Real Job, Marriage, New Lessons (1969-1970)

The first job I got was working on the building that housed a company called Syntex. It was a medication company that was just being built. I was used to working in the sun my whole life so I didn't stay there long. I wanted an inside job. I went to the Holiday Inn at Lucayan Beach. My boss, the bell captain, was a German. He hired me as a bellboy. I didn't like the job, but nothing else was available. As usual, I worked my way up and soon was able to work the bell captain's job when he was absent, sick, or traveling.

Shortly after, Mr. L. O. Pindlng became the leader of the Progressive Liberal Party (PLP)—a political party in the Bahamas. I was given the privilege of checking him into the hotel and showing him to his suite. At his arrival, I helped roll out the red carpet in front of the double door for his pleasure, but he took the side door instead. The boss told me I was his official bellman. When the vehicle pulled in, I moved closer and bowed to show honor as he came out. I offered to carry his hand luggage, but he said it was okay. The manager of the hotel and other dignitaries were on hand to welcome him. I told him I was his bellman and would accompany him to his room. I informed him that we had to go to the third floor so he allowed me to lead the way. I took him to his room, opened the door and let him in, checked everything to secure his safety, and then left. No, he didn't tip me.

I now tell myself, "Those were some good days." I made lots of tips from the people I helped and was able to save most of my money and buy nice clothes as was necessary. My biggest mistake, though, wasn't opening a savings account at a bank. My father told me to allow my aunt to hold my money for me. I didn't give his instructions a second thought, but did exactly as he said. He didn't know much about saving money at a bank. Most people back then kept their money at home, usually in their mattresses or in the loft.

I gave my aunt my payroll religiously every weekend. Luckily for me, I decided I would keep the tips myself, which worked out to be my only hope of having any money to bring home. My aunt told me she would use my money to buy groceries and household needs because I got paid before the others. She said she would replace it as soon as she got it from them. I didn't have any problem with that because I thought she would do as she told me. This arrangement didn't bother me, even though I understood that my roommates didn't want to come up with any money after satisfying their own needs. Of course, I figured that wasn't my fight. My aunt loved her brother, and she was saving my money like she said.

By the end of the year, I was ready to come home and show my parents how well I had done. The day for my departure came, and I asked my aunt for the money to bring home. She began acting as if she didn't know what I was talking about but said she had something for my father. When it was time for me to leave, she gave me this thick envelope for Baba. Thinking it was the money, I didn't question her any further. I took good care of it and protected it until I got home.

My parents were very glad to see me that afternoon so we enjoyed the evening together. The next morning, I gave Baba the envelope, feeling very proud of myself. He, too, was proud, seeing the fat envelope. You will remember, up to this time, I was working, but he collected whatever money I made. Neither he nor my stepmother told me what was happening to the money.

After giving him the envelope, I went out to visit my friends and see how they had been doing during my absence. When I got back home, the entire mood had changed. Baba called me over to where he was and started on my case. He threw his left hand at me, like he wanted to slap me. I didn't know what had gone wrong or what I had done to make them both so upset, especially Baba.

I managed to ask, "What's wrong?"

Baba was furious and made sure I knew it. "The next time you see the Bahamas, it will be on a map."

I was trying to find out what was the matter. He couldn't stand it anymore and blurted out, "The whole year you were in the Bahamas, you did not sleep in my sister's house once! You spent your money sleeping all over the place. Now you come with no money." I asked, "Is that what my aunt explained in that envelope? I was the only child she could find home in the evenings!"

I sat down and cried. I wasn't able to find anything else to bring satisfaction to myself. After I regained my composure, I tried to explain how things were and how I had managed to survive. Baba told me sternly "Please don't lie about my sister, she would never do anything like that." I knew in my heart she had done more because she told me on one occasion that I wasn't her brother's child. I kept that to myself.

I brought home thirty-five hundred dollars I had saved from tips after purchasing what I needed and gifts for my parents and friends. I gave Baba the three thousand dollars and kept the five hundred dollars for my pocket money.

When I handed him the money, I asked, "How do you think I was able to save this much just from tips if I were so bad about managing money?"

He was amazed to see me with this amount of money. "Where did you get this?"

I tried to explain about how one receives tips if the guest thought he performed well, but he was unable to understand it, never having heard of such a thing before. Nor did he believe my explanation.

He decided this was the leftover money from the rest I had already messed up.

He instructed me that I was on my way back to the boat to dive for lobster. I was a working man, but he assumed he was in control of me. I thought about that story for a long time, remembering how I was always the only one home to bring in the groceries when my aunt came in from the store. I remembered when I felt like having a fruit or a glass of juice or milk, there weren't any. I couldn't believe my parents, especially my father, could mistreat me so. For two long years, I was back in the boat because of this creative story my aunt put together. Any time I thought about it, I felt chills go down my spine, but I never allowed it to get to me or control me. I told myself I was used to or should have been used to these hard knocks. I looked to the Lord, knowing He knew I was speaking the truth. I tried to escape from going back to diving by seeking employment from Provident Ltd., but I was turned down. I consoled myself, resolved that I was still one of the best divers on the Caicos Bank.

My mistreatment went on the whole two years. I would work, and Baba collected the money. He bought groceries and the necessities for the household, but, if I needed a shirt or a pair of pants, I had to ask him or my stepmother. My father still had the *Wheeland Queen* with a dinghy boat and a six-horsepower engine astern, so life was a little easier than when I first started out in the boats.

In 1968, Mr. Lightbourne bought a two-ton pickup truck from Maguire in South Caicos and stayed there for a week to learn to drive it before bringing it home. He was the first native to own a vehicle on the island. He took passengers and everything else from place to place. Sometimes his son O'Neal (Cheese) and I took these trips with him, especially if he were taking passengers. The roads were still not good, and flat tires became a daily routine. We were equipped, though, with the necessary tools.

One particular day, we we had five flat tires, but to us, this was no problem. We had our two pieces of two-by-four, a big maul hammer, a handsaw, hand pump, patches, and holding cement. So we were back on the road in no time. We wanted our chance to drive the truck, but Gus didn't trust us, even though he wasn't the best driver. I learned to drive during my stay at Provident Ltd. before I went to the Bahamas. Cheese learned after his father got the truck. We didn't argue. We just quietly waited and contented ourselves fixing tires.

Gus also had a boat he built for himself, *Lady Cassius*. He used this boat to make many trips to South Caicos en route to Grand Turk. He would leave her in South Caicos and catch the MV *Sea Horse* to Grand Turk. We now had a phone on the island, located in the area of the little resort Mr. Luddington had built. He called it the Third Turtle Inn. He had a similar resort in the Bahamas that he called the Two Turtle Inn, in George Town Exuma.

On the return of one of Gus's trips to Grand Turk, he learned that his wife was sick and in need of a doctor. We had a nurse, but there was still need for a doctor. He was too tired to turn right around and take her to South Caicos, so he asked if I thought I was able to find South Caicos. I told him yes; confident I could, even though I had never gone on a small boat before. All my trips were on the sloops; still I thought I could find it. He said Cheese would go with me, and we organized the trip. Because he had a truck and an eighteen-horsepower engine, he had acquired a five-hundred-gallon tank to store gasoline for his convenience. We filled five six-gallon tanks to take with us. He usually took four but gave us one extra. We checked the anchor and ropes and made sure we had a bailer, some food, and water.

At seven on Sunday morning, we left for South Caicos with the two ladies. We made a nice bed in the bottom of the boat for Mrs.

Lightbourne and the nurse so they would be comfortable. As we pulled away, many people were on the beach, wishing us well. I was proud to be the captain of such a beautiful-looking boat with Cheese the engineer. She was fifteen feet long with a house in the center and just enough room in the back to seat two persons with one steering and the other looking out. As I think back now, I still think Gus built the prettiest boats in his day. Boy was I proud to be the captain. I felt bigger than Captain W. L. Swann.

At the onset of our journey, the weather was good, but as we got past Leeward Going Through, it got overcast and cloudy, like it was about to rain. I wasn't worried, though, because I knew the ladies couldn't get wet. Besides, Gus had two raincoats on board. Cheese and I put on our raincoats and braced ourselves for the worst. I was thinking my job was what mattered. The rain didn't come, but it got rough. The waves were breaking heavy. We could hardly open our eyes. As soon as one wave finished, another one came. Even though the ladies weren't getting wet, they could see us getting beat with the saltwater. They began to question whether I thought we could make it. I told them I was sure we would make it okay. I decided to stay close to land as we traveled. If we had to stop suddenly, we would be near land.

We didn't have any bathroom on board, and we had to stop to go ashore a few times for the ladies so they could be comfortable. The weather stayed uneasy the whole day, causing us to take twelve and a half hours. Normally, the trip was only five and a half hours long. As the sun was setting, we were on our last tank of gas. The ladies began to sing, so we felt good. I was encouraged because I had seen South Caicos just before the sunset. Knowing we were on our last tank of gas, as we drew nearer, I kept checking the tank by lifting it up to see how heavy it was. As we passed Milton Cay, I knew we were closer than ever but doubted the gas would hold out. I gave Cheese the wheel and took the gas tank in my hand, tilted it, and began to squeeze the bulb on the lead. We were almost there when I heard the engine make a sucking sound. I realized she was sucking air and squeezed faster. I heard another sound and knew the tank was empty.

I put it down and rushed forward, not knowing how close the rock by Christina Point was to the boat. I nearly broke my finger on that rock. We held on to it and guided the boat about another three hundred feet until we got to the dock. Thankfully, we made it!

We tied the *Cassius* to the dock, like seasoned seamen, and helped our passengers out onto the dock. I had to go look for someone with a vehicle to take Mrs. Lightbourne to the doctor's house since the clinic was closed on Sunday night. I ran into my friend Suputer Basden (Rough). He was driving a jeep and just getting off from work at the Admiral's Arms Hotel. He agreed to take the ladies to the doctor's and then took us to Highland, where the nurse's family was living. They looked after a big house called the Reeds House. We spent the night there along with the nurse.

We couldn't call back to Providenciales until eleven o'clock the next day because the one phone didn't operate until then. We didn't leave for Providenciales on Monday but filled our tanks with gasoline and left them in the boat. Back then, no one would stoop so low as to move other people's possessions. Later that day, we got a call that someone wanted us to bring back groceries so we went to Timco Ltd. Ltd. (the wholesale store), ordered the items, and asked that they deliver them to the dock. We loaded the boat that afternoon and left the next morning for home. We got there long before sunset. Well, if I don't live to be a hero again, I certainly was one then. Everyone, including me, was proud of my ability.

More and more people were purchasing vehicles. Some were giving up their land by ten and twelve acres for one car that sometimes didn't run for more than a month. Many people regretted their decisions later on. In 1969, an American businessman was one of the first to begin running charter flights between Providenciales, the Bahamas, and the United States. He soon became the regular airline. It soon became easier to fly with him than to go to South Caicos and catch Bahamas Air and then yet another flight to the United States. This was our only hope until Mackey International Airline started flying in the 1970s. Still, we depended on him because that airline only ran once a week and still had a stop in Grand Turk and George Town Exuma in the Bahamas before going to Miami.

We struggled with proper international airline connections until 1991. Many of us used this local airline even though we were packed in right along with the freight. We were even expected to carry packages on our laps according to how loaded the plane was. Sometimes we even sat on boxes just to get a seat. Other times, there was no air-conditioner or heater working. Even when the plane was loaded with building materials, the passengers were still satisfied, happy to get a flight.

After Air Florida came into Grand Turk, people still preferred to fly with the local airline Provo Air Service that Mr. Ed Hegner owned. At times, they would make reservations, and when they made it to Grand Turk by the scheduled flight, it was canceled or something. It would cost extra to come back home and wait for the next available plane. This happened to me more than once. Agents sometimes gave my seat to one of their friends.

To move freight on a large scale, we had two Bahamian boats coming to Providenciales from Miami via Nassau. For many years, Captain Moss and Captain Taylor owned these boats. That's how we got vehicles, heavy equipment, and materials. These boats made regular trips here for many years. They were very instrumental in bringing in those old cars traded for some of the people's best land.

I had great respect for my father and even more so for the way he held on to his land rather than letting it go cheap. He owned one hundred and sixty acres and never thought to give up one inch. My siblings and I still own that land today. People who sold their land for twelve dollars an acre are now seeing those acres go for thousands of dollars. Some of these people can't afford a house to live in now, and all their land is gone.

In 1969, when the Britannia Beach Hotel was completed, the owners were looking for good, hardworking men to fill positions. My uncle-in-law Archie Ewing was an employee there and told the boss he could get some capable men from Turks and Caicos who would work for her. He came home to select some men to travel back with him. Now earlier, my father told me that the only way I would ever see the Bahamas again would be on the map. Archie gave his boss nine names he thought would be able to go back with him. Herman Grant was one of these men, but his father didn't allow him to go. Parents wanted to keep their sons home, so they could control them and take whatever little money they made.

The eight men were ready to go, but Archie needed one more. He came to my father and asked about me going. Well, you can imagine what the answer was. Archie put up some good arguments on my behalf, but the answer was still no. Archie, however, was persistent and would not give up. At this time, Baba began to tell him why I wasn't going back. The truth was now coming out. In Freeport, Archie and his brothers stayed next door to my aunt. So he outlined the whole situation to my father who, until then, still believed that his sister was telling the truth and I was lying. Archie was my father's brother-in-law. He even explained how his sister-in-law told him I was the only child she could find after nine o'clock at night. He even expressed how he felt about the older brother working me on weekends in his business and never paying me. Then Baba believed.

He asked me why I didn't tell him, but he never gave me a chance to say. He now agreed to let me go, but Archie had to hold my money. Well, Archie stopped that right there and then. He told my father in no uncertain terms that, if I were old enough to work for the money, I could hold it myself. He reminded him that I was nineteen years old. Since the list of names Archie had left with his boss had Herman Grant on it, I went as Herman until we got that straightened out a few months later.

As in any developing country, the native men sometimes feel that the platter should be handed to them without any effort on their part. Some of the Bahamians were no exception, but Mr. Pindling set them straight as soon as he was elected prime minster. He encouraged all to improve their education, and he made the necessary provisions for each interested person to become qualified and take up employment.

We left home on Mr. Hilly Ewing's thirty-foot motorboat and broke down halfway to South Caicos. Because of that, we almost missed our flight on Bahamas Air. When we arrived in Nassau about seven thirty that evening, most of the men went in one immigration line. One of my traveling companions told me to accompany him in another line.

He said, "Sometimes when the officers are tired, they will carry you hard."

We got through okay. We spent the night at his daughter's house.

The next morning, we went to see Archie to find out about the plans for the day. We were informed that some of our men had slept in Fox Hill jail that night. The boss was supposed to meet us at the airport and bring documents from the Minister of Works Mr. A. D. Hanna so we would not have any problems, but that didn't happen. Later that day, we went over to Paradise Island to get documentation. We were taken from one office to another: personnel office, immigration office, and other offices. After we got our ID cards, we made our first visit to the hotel and enjoyed a complete tour of the buildings and grounds.

The next morning, we went house hunting. After a complete search, we narrowed our choices to four houses we thought we could use. On further investigation, we found two were too small and one was too old, but the last one was just right, just dirty. We decided we'd take it and went about cleaning and fixing it up. We cleaned the yard and floors, painted the walls inside and outside, and dusted and shined the furniture.

There was a man whom we thought to be sleeping, lying there in a corner the whole time, covered from head to toe. We discovered later that he was drunk. When we finished cleaning, we began to bring in our beds and furniture. This man, the owner, had given someone permission to rent the property on his behalf. He decided now was the time to rise and shine. We had already decided this house could do for the eight of us since one of the men of our company had gone to live with his daughter.

When we thought everything was going fine, the man got up and started degrading us as Turks and Caicos Islanders. He said he would never allow anyone from our country to take up residence in his house. He literally chased us out of his house and yard. He informed us that we were not used to anything good. The next day, we found a house in Key West Street that a Baptist minister owned. His church was on one side, and a barroom was on the other. We were allowed to set up house there and enjoyed our stay.

I worked at the Britannia Beach Hotel for a few months and then quit. I didn't like the job as a houseman and wanted something else. I left with them owing me one-week pay, ninety dollars. I left Nassau and went to Freeport. There I found a job at the Holiday Inn again, working as a security officer this time. Now this job I liked. It was a nice job. All of the officers got along well with each other, but I had some differences with the boss, a Trinidadian, so I left along with another officer, Charles Rolle, nicknamed Bill, who later became a good friend of mine.

Two days afterward, I got another job at a small hotel, Indies House, as a front-desk clerk. A week later, I ran into the same friend who told me about his job as a security officer at Island Security. My friend introduced me to the man who was hiring. I had worked with my friend before so he knew I was good. The boss asked if I had time to go to his office. When I came out of there, I was fitted with my full uniform, I had all my necessary forms filled out, and I was hired—all in twenty minutes.

That night, I went to work inside the EL casino. Later my friend walked inside and saw me on the job wearing my grey pants, white shirt, black tie, and blue jacket. He got jealous of me. I was working inside, and he was outside, which wasn't so nice. He thought the boss was going to hire me for outside the building as well. His uniform wasn't as formal as mine was. He wore khaki and not a coat and tie like me. He was envious and searched for the boss to complain. That very night, the boss, Bill Cuddy, had to take my friend to his office, give him the other uniform, and allow him to join me inside instead of outside. I worked at the casino until the end of 1971. I made good money and saved a good portion. I was promoted to supervisor, and my pay was increased, so I was happy.

I began saving my money just as I started working in Nassau. The first payroll we got, I went to the Canadian Imperial Bank and opened my savings account while the others stopped at the bar to get a "cool one." I was the first out of the nine of us to open a savings account. That night at home, they began to find out how I planned to save my money, and I told them I had opened a savings account. They questioned me about how to do it, and I explained it to them.

The next Friday, we came over the bridge and headed for the bank instead of the bar. I made my deposit and then stayed and helped them with theirs. After that, they made me their leader. If they didn't know something, they always thought I had the wisdom.

I started thinking about building my house. I needed advice about it. I solicited my cousin's husband, a carpenter, to help me since I lived with them at the time. He even obliged me by going to Miami to buy building materials for me because I couldn't get the time off. I paid for all the expenses of the trip, of course. In addition to the money I gave him to purchase materials, I sent ten thousand dollars to my father for him to begin digging the foundation and preparing for the building. At that time, no blocks were available so it was decided that the first phase would be built from rocks. They called it "tabby wall."

We hadn't started using house plans yet, so my brother-in-law built my house on the same principle as his: two bedrooms, one bath, an all-in-one kitchen and dining room, and a living room. The only difference was that he had an "A" roof and I had a "hip" roof. Everyone used zinc for roofing. By that time, we had investors and expats living on the island, and they introduced asphalt shingles. My house was the first with asphalt shingles. They had shingled a whole side of my house roof before they realized it wasn't the right way, so I had to live with that for a while.

My cousin-in-law shipped the materials from Miami to Grand Turk on a freighter, *San Antonio*. Baba called his nephew and had him clear the materials and keep them until he could get them. This nephew was sent money after he found out what the total cost was. In the meantime, Baba chartered the mail boat, which Mr. Algernon Dean owned, for about five hundred Jamaican dollars[7] to go to Grand Turk and bring the materials home for him.

While the materials were being transferred among Miami, Grand Turk, and Providenciales, someone changed the shutters. My father couldn't know because he hadn't seen them before. When I came

---

7 At that time, we were using Jamaican currency.

home to visit my parents and inspect the work, I brought brochures of the shutters and a list of what they should have received. I was amazed to see the cheap quality of windows and doors that were sent to my father. He called the nephew to find out about these differences and found out the windows and doors had been changed Supposedly the shutters arrived broken, and the carrier replaced them. My father found out, however, that his nephew was building at the same time and kept the good shutters for himself. He had a joiner in Grand Turk make cheap ones to send to my unsuspecting father in Providenciales. Later on, I prepared to go home again and asked a favor of another friend, to work for me until I returned.

I stayed home for two weeks before going back to the Bahamas, thinking I would be returning to my job. My friend told me he was tired of working outside in construction and wanted to keep that job because the air-conditioning was good. I just think he liked the salary. Rather than look for another job, I decided to come back home and supervise the building of my house. I closed my savings account and came back to Turks and Caicos.

In contrast to the Bahamas, there wasn't much to do socially at home. In Freeport, there was a wide choice of what to do each evening. Here though, the Third Turtle Inn was the only place to visit and have a drink before retiring in the evenings. Cheese and the rest of my friends were glad to have me home, and we would go to the Third Turtle often. One Friday evening, as we walked in, they slowed down like they were waiting for someone else. I didn't say anything, and they didn't explain. I didn't ask. At the bar, we ordered drinks, and I paid. When we got our drinks, they told me we could sit outside, and I agreed.

It was good to be back home with my friends, and we talked and laughed about nearly everything. Every time I laughed aloud, they would say to me, "Not so loud. We'll disturb the guests." I agreed, but I thought we were only having a social conversation.

I thought, *Why are they so cautious?*

When we went back inside to order a second round, I noticed everyone staring at us strangely. I thought they were trying to figure out who I was since I was new there and dressed differently. I had a medium Afro haircut and wore light blue bellbottom pants with a ¾ sleeve shirt, big collar, a scarf on my neck, jewelry, and high heel shoes. James Brown or Michael Jackson wouldn't have had anything on me.

No one said anything to us even though one could feel the discomfort. At nine forty-five, the bartender shouted last call for alcohol.

I asked, "Does the place close at ten?"

"No, eleven. You have to leave at ten."

I was puzzled about why we had to leave if we weren't ready yet and the expats could stay. I was sure we weren't disturbing the peace or the hotel guests. We weren't cursing or behaving badly.

I thought, *We should be able to stay as long as we are spending money.*

One of the boys said again that we had to leave the premises because we weren't going to get served any more. I was still trying to find out why and was informed it was the law. I wanted to find out whose law, the hotel's or the government's, but they didn't know. I reasoned that, as long as the doors were opened, we had a right to be served unless we were misbehaving, and we were not. I wouldn't let it drop.

I turned to the bartender this time. "Why can't we get served after ten?"

"It's the law so you better leave."

Well, I was beginning to get upset. "Or what!"

He answered enthusiastically, "I'll throw you out!"

Well, he didn't know that nobody spoke to me like that. I dragged him from behind the counter and asked, "Do I look like I should be spoken to in that manner? I am not in the category of persons you could speak to disrespectfully."

When I let him go, no one else said a thing to me. They were probably wondering among themselves who I was and where I came from. The boys left me there after the encounter with the bartender. I didn't know how to get to the main road, so I had to ramble through the bushes until I found it and then walked home.

I got home late, so I slept late the next day. After eating some breakfast my stepmother made for me, I looked for Cheese. He explained, "I did not want to leave you in the bar last night, Cracker, but the others insisted we leave. They were saying you came home with the Bahamian way; and that is only going to keep interested persons away from our country." I sat him down and explained to him that, "In the Bahamas, I could go to any church, school, theatre, club, or bar and stay until I was ready to leave. No law prohibited natives or blacks from going where they wanted to and allowing expats to stay and be contented."

In the earlier years, maybe a few places in Nassau wanted to establish such foolishness, but Mr. Pindling quickly changed that after he was elected as prime minister. So I wasn't used to this kind of mess, and I was sure not prepared to come home and sit under such oppression or racism. Here in Turks and Caicos, we didn't know what racism was exactly or how it felt until we were exposed to other races showing it. We heard a little about it from stories that people who traveled told of experiencing it firsthand. We always welcomed (and still do) anyone who came to our shores, but they must respect the natives they meet here.

Cheese said "Cracker, I understand the situation, but one of the boys with us is working up there. So, he is protecting his job. That's why he does not want to be identified with us." I thought that was too low to stoop, just to keep a job, when most of the brothers were looked down on.

The next night, Cheese and I went back to the bar. When the friends saw us, they gathered round but said nothing. We ordered our drinks, and the bartender told us we wouldn't be served. They had decided that I was a smart Bahamian getting into the business of the people of these islands, and they suggested I go back to where I came from. We didn't know what to do so we went outside to talk.

We sat at a table, and one of the guests came over and started talking to us. He offered us drinks, purchased them, and brought them out to us. When we started drinking them, someone came out of the bar and knocked our glasses over and out of our hands. Trouble started then. Cheese and I fought our way out of there that night back to back, protecting one another. Even our friends thought we were the ones looking for trouble and had found it. I found out right there and then that the people of Blue Hills don't stand together. But that didn't stop Cheese and me. We wanted to know why black people had to leave the hotel before ten while others could stay as long as they liked.

One policeman served as custom officer as well as immigration officer. The people at the inn complained to him about us coming up there, so he came to us and asked us to stay away from there or else he would have to arrest us. Because of his position, he could stay until he was ready to leave but no other black.

I asked, "What charges would you be able to bring?"

But he didn't say. Our reason for going around was to be able to socialize, meet visitors, and tell them about our beautiful island. But blacks were only needed to work and then were asked to leave the premises. To please these people, the government sent down other officers to investigate the story, and when they saw how natives were treated, they were offended.

Another night, I went there and met a new bartender. He looked familiar, but I couldn't recall where I had seen him before or how I knew him.

When he saw me coming, he came out from behind the bar. "Where do you think you're going?"

It got to the point where they didn't want us there at any time.

I said, "We only want a drink."

"You need to go back to the Bahamas where you came from."

"This isn't the casino," he said. "This is the Third Turtle."

Then I remembered where I knew him from. He used to come into the casino and gamble, knowing it was against the law for people living in the Bahamas to do that. That's where he knew me from because I had to throw him out of the casino for violating the law.

"What did you say? I'm the one home, and you're the one who needs to go back home."

He flew for me at that moment, and I had to teach him a little lesson in respect. A fight started, even among the guests who didn't like how these people were treating the locals. The next night, we went there and met some of the boys from the Bight there. They already had their first drink. They told us to sit back and relax because this was their night. They realized what Cheese and I were doing was to benefit everyone, and it would be unfair for all of them to sit back and allow only two of us to do the job. We appreciated their stand, and being tired, we went home. The next morning, we heard that the eight men from the Bight had been arrested.

There was a problem. There were only two small cells, so everybody was outside on the grass sitting down until they were later released. They sat on that grass all night. They could have gone home, but they were determined because they wanted this to stop before it got any further. They were tired of that kind of embarrassment. These scenarios went on until settlers to Providenciales recognized we were serious about equality. The managers decided to give me a job sometime in 1974.

Before that, I couldn't get a job anywhere. Some of my own people would tell the employers not to hire me because I was troublesome.

For a few months, I worked with Mr. Bob McElvy, who was in charge of the Shell gas station at South Dock and the airport. McElvy was a kind man to work with. He had three sons, and I was treated like the fourth. He was proud but kind. It was nothing to him to buy drinks for everyone he met in a bar. Because of that, some people didn't like him and decided he was a show-off. He had his own plane and often invited me to travel with him to the Bahamas or Miami. He looked at me not as an employee. He respected me as a man and a friend.

One day, an employer from the Third Turtle Inn asked me to come to their office. When I got there, they offered me a job as a bartender, which I accepted, but they also wanted me to keep other natives away from the property. I was very insulted at that offer and didn't try to conceal my feelings; I let them know how I felt about that. They still wanted me to work for them later, so I told them I would work and, if native people came to the bar, I would serve them. If they didn't know how to behave themselves, I would be the first to throw them out. On the other hand, though, if they were acting normal, having intelligent conversations, and relating normally, then they would be allowed to stay until the bar closed. That was the only condition on which I would accept the job. They understood, and we never had a problem again.

At this time, I was in a relationship with a beautiful young lady, Zenneth Swann. I had always dreamed that she would be my wife one day. Many other girls were in my life, but she was special. The boys would talk about all the other girls except Zen. They knew she was my girl. My mother told me that, when I was born, Zen's mother came to see us. She was then pregnant with Zen. A month later, Zen was born, and we went to see them. Mommy said she held my face close to Zen's face and told me to kiss my wife. Well, as I grew, I got to know her and always liked her, but her father was a boat captain, and her family was well off. He thought I was just another poker, but as time passed, I tried getting close to her.

One day after school, she was walking home by herself. I took that chance to say something to her.

She told me, "Find your kind."

"Well, I have always found my kind, and that's why I'm talking to you."

Little episodes happened until she got the message. We fell in love in 1966. At that time, I was only able to see Zen standing by the door of her house if I passed by in the road or at church. We couldn't talk openly after her parents found out we liked each other. I guess it was all right when we were little, but when we became teenagers, things changed. This made me like other girls, and of course, they liked me.

At one time, only twelve girls were on the island besides my cousins, and they all liked me. The boys got mad, but they didn't do anything because they knew what would happen. In 1970, I was in the Bahamas and didn't write Zen for a while. I guess she thought I had left her. Someone came from home and told me that some of her relatives were trying to put her and another guy together. I decided to come home for a week or two to find out what was happening. Now in those days, tailor-made suits were the norm, and Aramis cologne was the hottest thing on the market. Everybody in the Bahamas was wearing it, but it wasn't on the island yet.

I always liked coming home on the weekend because that's when most of the activities were held. Bahamas Air's schedule worked out well too. We would fly to South Caicos and then catch Caicos Airways or Air Caicos to Provo. On this particular trip, the flight was a little late, so by the time we got into Providenciales, it was just getting dark. There were no lights on the airstrip, but the pilot still could see well enough to land the aircraft. On our arrival there was a woman with her son waiting to see if she had a package on the flight. She dropped me home without waiting for me to pay her.

My stepmother was just leaving to go to the Federation House for an ice cream sale. She was surprised to see me because I hadn't let anyone know I was coming. That was so neither Zen nor the boy would know I was home until I showed up. I stopped home long enough to get cleaned up and went where I knew everyone was having a good time. When I walked in, they were doing an exercise, "Three-Step Dance." Everyone stopped and looked at me. My cologne lit up the room, and I received more hugs and kisses than I needed.

When I looked toward the window, I saw Zen and her relatives sitting down. Someone was outside the window standing up. I figured it was the guy. Well, I had a lot of fun with lots of girls. I talked to everyone else except Zen. When everything was over, I was walking down the road with another girl after Zen and company had left, and we soon caught up with them. The boy was trying to get a word across.

I moved in and told her, "You belong to me, so tell that boy to get lost. I will see you tomorrow."

The next day, she was walking down the road looking around. I saw her, but she didn't see me. I dodged around this and that as I walked along until I got to where she couldn't see me. Then I came up behind her and greeted her. She almost had a fit. She couldn't believe I was behind her and never saw me coming. I talked with her a while, stole a kiss, and left. I don't think she talked to that boy ever again.

All the while, I was involved with other girls, and they were becoming serious about me, but I had given my word to Zen. During our engagement, I had two beautiful daughters with another girl. There was so much turmoil about this. I was very confused and didn't know what to do. I think I got involved with other girls because the only place Zen frequented was church since her parents were Christians. There were no phones for us to call, and I didn't like to write while I was in the Bahamas. Zen thought I didn't care. During church services, we looked at each other so much that I don't think we ever heard what the preacher had to say. During the pregnancies, I was very scared of what might happen. To make matters worse, people were bringing tales of what the father of the other girl would do to me. I was worried all the time.

Just before I started working for McElvy, I was working with a local contractor, Mr. Samuel Lightbourne, who was building Blue Hills Primary School. Two of my friends came on the job and called me. I was down in the catchment tying steel. When I raised my head and saw them, I went over and talked with them. They were sitting in a car. As I came close, they told me they had been in the other district and my girlfriend had told them to bring two bottles of Heineken beer for me because she knew the sun was hot and I would like something cold. I felt they were lying but took the two short bottles, thanked them, and went back to work. This happened on a Monday morning, July 24, 1972, at about eleven thirty in the morning. When I got back on the job, the supervisor asked for one, and another guy asked for the other one. I gave them both away even though I wanted a cold one badly. Later though, they started complaining about aches in their stomach, and then they started going for bathroom breaks quickly.

The next morning, we were already on the job when we heard people crying not too far from where we were. We dropped our tools and went to see what was going on. There we found out that someone had just died in childbirth. She was a girl I knew, so I tried to get close to the window until I could see her lying there. After a while, my supervisor came over, and we went down the road to the snack bar. He ordered a cheeseburger and asked if I wanted anything but I didn't.

"I'm not hungry."

At that time, I was very careful where I ate and whom I took food from because there were many threats made against me. As I sat there waiting for the supervisor, these same two boys came to me again. They called me outside, and I went to see what they were up to. One of them showed me a joint.

Yes, I had tried marijuana once or twice in the Bahamas, and after coming home, I tried it again but wasn't really into it. There were times in South Caicos or Grand Turk when I found a joint and brought it back, searched for the boys, and shared it. Most of the times, it wasn't enough to make anybody high. We just sat around laughing at each other. One night, about five of us were on our way to the Third Turtle when we discovered one of the boys had a joint. As we walked down the steps to the entrance, we lit up. By the time we walked into the bar, we were all laughing and didn't know why. People looked at us funny, probably thinking we were crazy, laughing every minute.

This particular day, though, the substance these boys had really didn't look like what I knew it should. I asked if they were not tired of going into the bushes and getting bad leaves to smoke. With that, I went back inside. One of them came after me, sat beside me, and lit up the joint.

He held it out to me. "If you don't believe me, try it."

I didn't want to do it, but they were my best friends or pretending to be. I took it, put it to my lips, and tasted it but didn't inhale.[8] This joint tasted bitter on my lips so I gave it back to him. "I'm not interested."

He went back to the car, but they didn't leave. Suddenly I felt like I didn't know where I was or what was happening to me. My supervisor was there so I tried telling him that I wanted to go home. I became sleepy then and couldn't feel a thing. I got scared. I walked outside, trying to control myself. I looked out to the horizon but couldn't distinguish the sea from the sky. These boys were watching

8   People laughed when President Clinton said he didn't inhale, but it could happen because it happened to me.

me, asking me what the matter was. They offered me a ride home, pretending they didn't know what was wrong with me. I went with them, though, because I didn't have a choice.

As we rode toward my house, we happened to pass the house where the dead girl was. I felt like I was going through a dark tunnel that got darker and hotter as we got further into it. As we passed the house, I could hear singing like I never heard before. Approaching the gravesite, I heard people crying. I moved further into the tunnel. I could hear people begging for forgiveness and mercy. They sounded like they were ahead of me down in a hole. I couldn't see them, but I could see redness from the fire and feel the heat. I felt like I was going to fall in the hole, and I screamed. Just then, they announced I was home. They didn't take me up in the yard like they should have. Instead, they dropped me off in the street and left as soon as I jumped from the car. I looked around and started up the hill toward the house. I could see three persons standing by the window in my house. I looked across the yard toward the Bethany Baptist Church to regain my focus and then looked back at my house. I was thankful no one was there and continued walking toward my father's house. When I got inside, my stepmother was cooking, cleaning, and crying.

She asked, "Did you hear about the girl who died?"

"Yes, but I don't feel like talking. I want to get to bed."

She had a relative's son living with us. He was still small, so I held his hand and asked him to come with me in the room. I thought for the first time in my life that I was scared. As I entered the pantry, to pass through to my room, the living room seemed brightly lit. I knew we were only using kerosene lamps because we didn't have electricity yet, but there was no light as bright as that. In my amazement over the light, I looked around. The dead girl with her baby in her arms was lying there. I started to run back in the kitchen, but the voice said, "Charlie, come here. I have something to tell you." I froze right there. The little boy ran back when he sensed I was afraid. He became afraid as well. By then, everything went dark, but I still could hear her voice. She explained that she hadn't died naturally and said, if I had drunk those beers, I would have died along with her.

When I heard that, I screamed. Ma Tiny rushed in to see what had happened. I told her how I was just listening to this dead girl and saw her and her baby. At first, she thought I was crazy, but the whole time while they were preparing for the funeral, I was communicating with that girl. After her burial, I began to catch myself. I met the house filled with people. I was sweating heavily. Ma Tiny told me that she used about six bath towels trying to keep me dry, but that didn't stop the water from pouring out of my skin. My grandmother was there, and she rubbed me down with garlic mixed with turpentine and burned candles with the idea of keeping away evil spirits.

The majority of my people in Providenciales always had ill feelings toward me, and when I decided to build my house, it got worse. What made it worse was that I came home wearing the latest styles in clothing. The shops here were small, so the variety was limited.

My father had just bought a nine-year-old car, a 1963 Impala Chevrolet with white exterior and blue interior, the best looking on the road. Compared to the others, it was practically new. Because of my status, all of the girls liked me so I had to be very careful. People looked at me like I was a stranger from a different planet. Sometimes I wondered if I were really so different. The way people hated me, I felt like I was. That's why, after I caught myself and revived from that episode, I asked the Lord to keep me away from drugs as far as possible and, if I used them again, to take my life.

As for friends, I never trusted anyone again. I still find it hard to trust friends. Those guys were supposed to be my best friends! After this sickening incident, one couldn't bear to remain on the same island with me, so he left the island and made his abode in the United

States. He became very shy of me and did his best to keep away from me. The other turned to alcohol.

Things got worse after the babies. Many people told me different tales of my fate. Sometimes I used to think these people were being paid to make me a nervous wreck. I was still working for McElvy when Zen got pregnant at the end of that same year. A terrible situation got worse. Mc Elvy was even threatening that he would be hurt seriously if he didn't fire me first. People were asking about my intention and warned me to be careful. My parents questioned my sanity as they asked how I got myself into such a mess. Well, I was engaged to Zen, so I thought it was the right thing to do to marry her since she had waited for me all this time. She was special. When I decided to get married, my house wasn't quite finished so my parents said we could live with them until it was completed.

We were married on April 29, 1973. I wasn't quite ready because I was broke at the time, and I had always felt that a man should be financially fit before he got married, but our situation was different. We were unable to relax and take a honeymoon. If Zen's father hadn't given her three hundred dollars, I would have had to go to work the next day.

The wedding was on Sunday afternoon. While I was getting dressed to be married, I hardly knew myself because I was afraid I would die during the ceremony, as people were saying would happen. My legs were supposed to buckle and give way under me beside Zen. I honestly thought it would happen so I was really nervous. I was unable to put on my bow tie. My father had to help me with that. Finally, I was ready. On my way to the Federation House, I prayed as never before, and I made it through the ceremony at the Federation House. In those days, if a girl got pregnant before marriage, the couple wasn't allowed to marry in the church building. I am not sure what the significance of that rule was, but we lived by it.

When we pulled up to the Federation House, it was packed with people, most of who were there to witness me dropping dead. As I got out of the car, people gathered around me, some out of pity or sympathy and others out of curiosity, wanting to make sure they witnessed my death. I walked up to where the pastor was waiting and waited for Zen, who arrived shortly afterward with her father, who walked with her and handed her over to me then we finished the walk back to the pastor together. She was very beautiful, but I didn't tell her because I felt like I wasn't going to live to enjoy pleasurable days with her.

The ceremony started, my legs began to shake, and I began to sweat. I was too afraid to look around.

Reverend Woosley asked, "Will you have this woman to be your lawful, wedded wife?"

I stopped and thought for a while. "I will."

This was supposed to be the time when I died. Well, nothing happened. I could hear some people exclaiming, "He is still standing!" Others were reassuring themselves, "It will soon happen." The ceremony continued, and the pastor pronounced us husband and wife. Still nothing happened. I began to feel a small flicker of relief. At the point where he told me I could kiss my bride, I looked at her and thought in my heart, *Woman, this may be my last kiss, but I'm going for it.* Her parents came and congratulated us, followed by my parents. As the others were drawing near, I told Zen, "Let's get out of here."

We tried to press through the crowd and headed for the blue Mustang that Tom Lightbourne, our chauffeur for the day, was driving. We drove around for a while and then went back to the Federation House for the reception. I wasn't really settled until we finally went home after the reception. The next day, we couldn't rest. Every half while, someone came to visit us. Some I allowed to come to our room, some I stopped at the door, and others I went out to speak with. I couldn't let my guard down. I didn't know who was friend or foe and didn't dare take any chances.

On Monday evening, there was a wedding party at the Federation House. I didn't attend because I was still too nervous to be in the crowd. This was especially so after a woman came to visit us in the evening. When I heard her, I got a feeling she wasn't someone I wanted to see, so I told her to wait a while because I was changing my clothes. She insisted I look to the door, and as I opened the door, she reached out for me and grabbed me like she wanted to drag me out of the door. I moved out of her way and closed the door quickly. In her eyes, I could see something telling me to stay away from her. She shouted out that, even though I was running away from her, I couldn't run for long because she was going to get me. Then everything went silent, so I looked out, and she was gone. I couldn't understand her actions, and neither could my wife, who asked me what I thought she meant. I had to admit I didn't know, but I knew I had to be careful, especially with her.

Not very long after that, we heard noises in the street that we could distinguish as excitement that wasn't happy. Soon someone came by the house and told us that that same woman had just gotten killed in a road accident. Some boys were driving a truck up the road, and she got knocked down. It wasn't known whether she wasn't paying attention or the truck was speeding, but she was gone. The news made me feel lighter, like I had just gotten rid of a heavy load.

The next week, I got sick to my stomach and kept feeling worse. I could hardly eat anything. I was still afraid. It seemed everyone was going to Haiti trying to kill me. I was so sick that I ended up in Grand Turk Hospital with what the doctor said was an ulcer. I stayed in the hospital for four days but didn't see or feel any improvement. I spoke to the doctor about this, suggesting that I would like to go to the Bahamas to seek medical attention if they couldn't do anything for me. He told me, if I wanted to do that, just do it, making sure I understood clearly what he meant. He wasn't giving me any letter of information to take with me or any referral. I decided to go anyway and asked the matron of the hospital if I could use the telephone to get a message to my wife and let her know about the decision I had made. The matron insulted me, saying the people of Providenciales knew nothing about using telephones because we didn't even have any. That was how she spoke to me, and that was the general attitude of most people in Grand Turk against the people of the Caicos Islands. They looked down on us.

One nurse there, Cynthia Simmons-Astwood, knew me. She rebuked the matron and allowed me to use the phone. At that time, we still only had one telephone in Turtle Cove, so I told the person at the station to get a message to my wife so she could come to the phone to speak to me. Two hours later, I phoned back, and my wife was there waiting. I informed her of my intent to travel even though we didn't have any money. The flight was for the next day, and I wanted to be on it so I told my wife to explain the situation to my parents. The next day, my wife and her mother flew to Grand Turk to see me before I left. She brought some money that she had gotten from her parents and my father. Nurse Astwood even helped me get reservations, secured the letter from the doctor, helped purchase the ticket after my wife came with money, and helped to prepare me to travel.

As I was leaving the hospital, the doctor told me that if I died, he wasn't to be blamed. He was angry because he was forced to write the letter to the doctor in Nassau or risked being reported to the authorities. I said I might have died if I didn't leave that place. Nurse Astwood went to the airport with me to see me off. My wife was also there along with her mother. I respected that nurse for the way she stood up for me in my time of need.

When I arrived in Nassau, I went to live with my brother-in-law Wendell Swann and saw the doctor, an Indian doctor from Jamaica, the next morning. After my examination, he told me that I didn't have an ulcer but that I had a nervous stomach nervous stomach that would have developed into ulcers if I didn't seek help when I did. He said I had to come in and see him every two weeks to complete the treatment. That was impossible since I lived in Turks and Caicos. I expressed that to him, and he suggested I look for a job there so I could complete the treatment. Since I had told him the whole story of my life, he also thought it would do me good to be away from home for a while. I discussed it with my wife, who agreed.

One day, I was walking down Bay Street with nothing to do, so I walked out to Prince George Dock. A four- mast schooner of one of the fleet was tied up to the fleet of the Wind Jammer Cruise. A thought immediately raced through my mind and began speaking to the men there.

I asked, "Are you looking for crewmembers?"

They responded, "What time could you be ready to start working?"

Of course, I quickly told them, "I am ready anytime—like now." They said: "We are sailing this afternoon, so get your stuff ready." I inquired: "Where do you sail, and how often do you come back to Nassau?" They replied: "We sail around the Bahama Islands and return to Nassau every two weeks." That was ideal for me, but when I asked about the pay, I was disappointed. Starting pay was eighty dollars a month, and raised to one hundred dollars a month after two weeks.

After I started the job, I realized why I got hired so quickly. The owners brought no milk or juice for the crew, and the food wasn't good. Bahamians only stayed for the first few months and then left. The only persons who stayed on were some West Indians who were far away from home and wanted a job to survive, something like myself. I used to wonder how passengers enjoyed those cruises because the service got worse. As soon as we got to the dock, we crewmembers would buy fresh milk, juice, ice cream, and a good meal.

I stayed for three months because I had to visit the doctor every two weeks. I was only able to pay my doctor bill and write Zen. I wasn't making enough money to do anything else. In fact, Zen sent me money that her parents and my parents put together. They also took care of her in my absence.

One morning while still on the boat, I was sleeping on deck along with one or two of the crewmembers. I fell asleep and started dreaming. We were tied up at the dock in Nassau. I dreamed that my first child had died so I was crying in my sleep. One of the men nearby woke me. I told him my dream and then remembered my wife was just about ready to deliver. I rushed to the telephone but realized it was too early to call the community phone. We still didn't have any personal phones then. I went back to the boat and waited until after ten before going to make the call. I found out I was the father of a baby boy we named Wayne. I felt like I was the biggest man on that cruise for the whole week. I decided then that I had to do some real work, so I jumped off the ship in Freeport when we got in port to look for a better job.

I lived with my cousin, who was like a sister to me and her husband who was like a father. I was in Freeport for two weeks before I got a job, but they didn't mind. It was a good-paying job with Bahamas Security, and I enjoyed the time I spent with that company. One Sunday afternoon in February 1974, I was making ready for work when I heard a horn blowing outside. I looked out and saw a black Cadillac pulling in the driveway. It was a taxi, and the driver was calling me. It was time for me to go to work so I continued to make ready. I was combing my hair and putting on my tie when I heard the front door slam. I looked outside and saw my cousin reaching into the car and take out this beautiful baby. She began to call me. So now I started paying attention and rushed outside. When I got to the outside, I saw this handsome, bright-skinned baby boy with long, curly black hair and bright eyes. I wondered whose baby he was as I started to go closer. My cousin turned to me and exclaimed that this beautiful baby was mine, and she handed him to me. As I held out my hands for him, his eyes lit up as if he knew me or knew I was his father.

As I kissed him, I saw Zen inside the car and asked "Why did you come to Freeport?" She replied, "I came because I was not hearing from you as often as I should, and I miss you." She came during her midterm break. She was a teacher at Blue Hills Primary School, now Oseta Jolly Primary School. She began teaching in January 1969. I was very surprised and at a loss for words because she hadn't let me know they were coming.

My boss was, by this time, sitting there in his car waiting for me to go to work so I couldn't stop too long. I kissed her and told her I would see her later. I went to work, but I wasn't functioning too well. I could only think of my handsome son.

The next morning was my day off from work, and my cousin said I could use her car after I drove her to work at the Royal Bank of Canada. So I dropped her off, went back, and had breakfast with Zen. She said the baby needed some stuff, but she wasn't ready to go out yet. She wanted a little more sleep, so she dressed him, and I took him with me to the bank. I wanted to get some money so we could buy what he needed. My cousin must have already told them about how handsome my son was because, when I walked in with him, all those girls in the front left their workstations and came to see my baby. I kept reminding them not to hurt him because each one wanted to hold him. They made such a commotion that the manager came out to see what the matter was and restored order. I was glad to hurry out of there.

We went back to the house, picked up Zen, and then went shopping. I encountered the same kind of reaction in the stores as in the bank. Everyone wanted to touch him, hold him, or stand and watch him. I was proud to be his father. Zen and Wayne stayed with me for a week and then went back home. I stayed on in the Bahamas and decided in July to go home to be with my family and get my house finished.

One morning, I was preparing for a trip to Grand Turk when a member of staff from the Third Turtle Inn came to tell me that management wanted to talk to me. I stopped at the inn on my way to the airport for a quick chat with the manageress, Mrs. Donna Bartram. She said she had a vacant position and could give it to me if I were going to be home for a while. When I found out what the position was, I told her that, while I used to drink scotch and ginger ale, I didn't know how to mix it so that should tell her about my bartending knowledge. She said that was no problem to her because she had already decided to teach me.

I went to work the next Monday from eight in the morning until closing time. Then I had to clean up, stock the bar from the stock room across the bridge, and transport ice from across there as well before going home. On Saturdays, I worked from three in the afternoon until closing, around midnight or one. A few of the folks there who knew me from the earlier days looked at me puzzled-like when they saw I was working, but never said much. As soon as they got to know me personally, we became friends. I assumed they knew the saying, "You should always be nice to a cook, a bartender, and a doctor."

I liked my job. The boss showed me how to mix some drinks and then gave me a bartender's guide that was very helpful. I studied it well, and before long, I was mixing forty-five drinks from memory. Some of the staff members who were there before me became very critical of me, but the boss was proud of the job I was doing so I didn't concern myself with them. I was having a good time getting to know the Luddingtons, Wards, and Mrs. Bartram. She taught me much about hotel business during her short managerial period. Then the Peacocks took over.

Shortly after he came, Mr. Peacock called me into his office and told me how he had been watching me. I thought he was going to fire me, so I began trying to think what I did or didn't do to bring this on. But instead, he told me he was thinking of making me a supervisor. I was really shocked and surprised, but I didn't refuse. I took on the challenge and did my best. Some of the other employees resented me, but I only wanted them to do their jobs and keep the hotel running smoothly. I tried to be nice to everybody, but never got too friendly anymore, so people started calling me proud, especially after I moved up to supervisor.

All this time, we were still living at my father's because my house wasn't yet finished. I could see that Ma Tiny was getting tired of us being there, even though she promised we could stay there as long as we wished or had to. A couple weeks into the marriage, her attitude changed. Some days, she showed it more than others. At times, she would comment about not having enough air inside.

We were happy to establish our home when the house was finished. At that point, I could celebrate my life because I was still alive. I had learned not to worry about the threats, but I was still careful whom I took food from and even how to protect my drinks. Since I'd been a young man, I always made sure I had pocket money even though Baba controlled my money. If I asked him for something, he always gave it to me. My father was always careful where he ate also, so I learned that from him. As a child, I would see him visit friends, and when he was offered food, he would refuse, saying his wife had just fed him. Sometimes I would know that she hadn't even lit the fire for the day.

We used to have some wonderful times, making music and keeping our culture alive. Cal Dalton, during his visits here, used to join us on the banjo, Fuller Walkin (Big Link) played the guitar, Bob Callug played bass, and I was on the piano. The bass was a tub with a nylon line through the bottom in the center of the tub fastened on a piece of wood. When we started, we would have everyone dancing. We played songs like "Shame and Scandal," "Island Woman," "Yellow Bird," "Matilda," "Island in the Sun," and "Provo Farewell." I enjoyed myself. The people in my group had fun, and the onlookers were happy, so I don't know where the thing about me thinking I was better than others came from.

This feeling of resentment toward me increased after I got another promotion to assistant manager. Some people were saying I didn't know what I was doing or I had never finished school. They thought they or their educated relatives should have the position. I think it was because they badmouthed me so much that it made me more aware of my responsibilities and caused me to perform even better.

Another small hotel wasn't too far from the Third Turtle Inn, the Erebus Inn. Mr. Peacock was asked to manage this hotel as well. He, in turn, put me in charge of it, commenting that he knew I could do it. I wasn't too sure, but I was willing to try it. I managed it for one year and eight months. By this time, we had another baby, a girl we named Pamela. We lived at the Erebus and hired a babysitter for Wayne and Pamela while Zen was in school. The hotel had given me a truck to drive, so I guess that was too much for me, according to my fellow islanders. I believe I was the first native manager, and I had the privilege of meeting many officials and executives.

In my spare time, I studied hotel, motel, and restaurant management by correspondence course via International Correspondence School (ICS). My wife studied along with me, and I think things were going very well at the Third Turtle and Erebus. After some time, Mr. Peacock was asked to manage another small hotel, the Evans Inn in Grand Turk. A native had built this hotel and then sold it to someone else. It was a nice place but didn't attract many guests. I suppose it was too far from the beach even though it had a beautiful view. Mr. Peacock sent a gentleman there who he thought could make it go, but that didn't happen. One day around lunchtime, he came up the Erebus hill, and I could see he had something on his mind. He asked my wife and me to have lunch with him and his wife and told us during the meal that he would like for me to manage it. I thought for a while about the changes that would take place in my family if I had to move to Grand Turk. I didn't want to live over there and leave my family here. Even if I took my wife, we would have to leave our two children. He continued to state his position and his desire for me to try it. Finally, I accepted his appointment reservedly.

I went to Grand Turk to see what I could offer and what results would come forth. When I got there, the person I was supposed to take over from picked us up at the airport and took us to the inn and introduced us to the cleaner who lived there to look after the place. He explained I would be taking over from him and managing the place. She started cursing and picking up her belongings to leave. She informed him that she would never be caught dead working under a Caicos man. She was serious. She was insulted and very angry that they could bring a man from Caicos to be her boss. I don't know if it was because I was black or just a Caicos man. She left that place as fast as she could.

After I got settled there, I advertised open positions. I hired some pleasant people, and we had a good working relationship. We stayed there for a few months while our parents kept the children for us. We missed them terribly and longed to be with them. We were unable to call them because there were still no phones in homes in Providenciales yet. I didn't think I could make it that long without my beautiful babies.

Things began to go wrong at the Third Turtle and Erebus Inn. The owners probably thought Mr. Peacock was spending too much time with the natives and trying to promote and help them. They wanted to get rid of him. There were many different stories and rumors, but I wasn't getting any word from my authorities. Every time I asked about payroll, no one at the home office knew anything, so I quit and went back home. Mr. Peacock went to Grand Turk to take over the inn and told me that when he got the whole mess straightened out, he would send for me again. Before they got anything worked out though, he was forced to leave the island. I didn't go back to Third Turtle. Instead, I went back to diving for lobster for a short while.

On October 17, 1977, our third child was born, another beautiful girl named Vanessa. The morning Zen went into labor, I was making ready to go in the boat for a week. I took the two other children to their aunt. I was still preparing to go fishing, but my mind kept thinking I should stay with Zen. Even so, I still got on the truck to go to Five Cays where we kept the boat. As we passed the clinic where Zen was, I told my old man I wanted to stay with her because anything could happen. He insisted I go, saying someone would let me know the next day what happened. I was hurt that he still wanted to rule me even though I had a family. The whole time I was at the hotel, it was all right, but now, working in the same dinghy with him, he felt he was boss.

I jumped off that truck and told him, "Hell no! Not today. I am a man, and that's my wife. And I'll be with her until she delivers."

I didn't go in the boat anymore that week. I stayed home and attended to the baby. I was getting tired of fishing though, so in January 1978, one of my cousins and I went to the United States to look for work. We got a free flight out with one of my friends, who I got to know while working at the hotel. He had a plane and dropped us off in West Palm Beach, Florida. We caught a bus to Ft. Pierce. The next day, we started looking for jobs. Everywhere we went, we were asked for our Social Security numbers. Well, we didn't have one, so we ended up picking fruits in the orange groves. It wasn't the easiest job. In fact, it was rough. Some Bahamians were in these groves from the contract days when the United States used to recruit people to pick fruits and vegetables. They just did that and nothing else. Some had been there for years and still didn't have a house of their own, a car, or even a savings account. The pay was small.

I used to smoke then and couldn't afford a pack of cigarette some days. One particular day, I didn't go to work and wanted a pack of cigarettes. There was no one else home for me to borrow money from so I found myself picking up the used cigarette butts and rolling them to make a cigarette so I could get a smoke. Vanessa was our baby then, and I think she had the hardest life as an infant. We were unable to provide for her as we should. By then, Zen wasn't teaching. She left during the time I was at the hotel, so our income was really small. The day I had to pick up cigarette butts to make a homemade cigarette for me, I decided there must be a better way. I bought a ticket for Zen to come visit me in Florida and do a little shopping before we would go home. She brought Pamela with her on the trip. I don't think we paid airfare for children under three years old then. I made good friends in Ft. Pierce and knew I would miss them when I left.

We used to go out together on Friday nights. On Saturday mornings, we would go to each other's homes for breakfast or lunch. One Friday afternoon, I bought some nice Nassau grouper, cleaned it up nicely, seasoned it, and left it for the next day for home-style boiled fish and grits. My cousin and I lived together. He went to work for a few hours that morning. He and I took turns cooking, but we looked after our own room. This was my time to cook, so I fixed his up and put it aside before I gave the other boys theirs. About six of them were eating when my cousin came in. He walked right into his room without saying anything. When he came back out, however, he informed me that he didn't come to the United States to feed the whole town. He had a family back in the islands to look after.

Well, the boys laughed because they thought that was mean. We ate at everyone else's house without any problem. Because they laughed, he came after me and punched me in my chest. I know Mike Tyson can't punch as hard as he did. I had chest pains for several weeks. When I saw how angry he was and knew he was about to hurt me, I retaliated with two left jabs and a straight right. At this point, the boys stopped us, and we didn't speak to each other for weeks. But I felt like something was broken in my chest. I had to cough to regain my composure. I thought the refrigerator was broken because that's where he landed. One day after we got home from work, I heard a knock on my room door. My cousin was coming to make up. I didn't wait for him to say anything. I missed him, so I asked, "Why did we have to fight all this way from home, as good as we lived for so long; we are now fighting for grits and fish? I think we could do better." He was just waiting to apologize because he said, "I miss you too, I am sorry." We hugged each other then, and we remembered that incident for a big joke afterward.

Moving back home, jobs were not so forthcoming. I thought about getting into the taxi business. At that time, quite a few small planes were touching down on the small airstrip we had. I felt that if I had a car, I could make enough money to feed my family. I didn't have enough money to purchase a car though. I went to Mr. Art Butterfield, one of our local businessmen, and tried to set up a deal. He owned a small supermarket and gas station. He had a 1968 Ford station wagon that he wasn't using, so I asked if he would allow me to use it to taxi in. He thought at that time the taxi business couldn't pay a taxi driver and the car owner, so he suggested I borrow some money and purchase the car so I could own it. Well, I wasn't in that position, so he signed as surety for me to get the loan. I appreciated the effort he made to help me and did my best to make my payments on time.

After some time though, I started getting many troublesome days from that wagon and spent more money keeping it on the road than I could save. I was in the mechanic shop every day trying to get something fixed. One day, the mechanic Mr. Phil Ran got angry and asked me why my car was so different from everybody else's. At times, I would take my car out of the shop and not even reach the main road before it broke down. I would have to walk back to the shop and ask them to come check it again. They always had to pull it back in the yard.

The second nuisance was flat tires. I had flat tires so often that it almost became my second name. It seemed I was getting flat tires three times a day. I grew a real dislike for Mohawk tires ever since. I would buy one tire one day and have to replace it the next. After purchasing them from the same place, they started offering me the second at half price. The owner of the mechanic shop felt so sorry for me that, on one of his trips to Florida, he bought me four six-ply Goodrich tires at a good price. We put those tires on, and then everyone started talking about how good they looked.

A few nights later, I went to play dominoes and parked my car on the side of the road. When it was time for me to leave, the four tires had been slashed with a knife. I was angry, hurt, fearful, and disgusted. If I had known who did it that night, the people would have sung "In the Sweet Bye and Bye" for him or them. That's how I felt while riding home on rims. The next morning, I had to go back to those Mohawks again. Mr. G. Thomas felt so sorry for me that he lent me a car to taxi in while mine was in the shop. I had reason to rent a car later just so I could keep my customers. On one occasion, I rented a car and left for a meeting in Grand Turk that evening. I called the shop and asked them to have someone pick it up from the airport. The employee they sent for the car found out it was filled with gasoline, so he took his friends joyriding until it was empty and had to leave it on the road. Then some wisecrack thought he would burn it down, and since I had it, I would have to pay for it.

The country had just entered into the two-party system of government with the People's National Organization (PNO) and the People's Democratic Movement (PDM). I was attending a meeting of the PNO when one of the attendees' wives called him to let me know that the car had gotten burned down. She also said I had to be careful when I go back to Providenciales because some guys were putting together a gang to beat me up when I got back.

I thought, *That would be the day.*

I got back home expecting to have trouble, but everyone was quiet, so I kept quiet. They were disappointed when they found out I had already turned that car in.

The day I got my car out of the shop, I headed to the airport in search of a job. A single-engine Cessna 210 came in with just the pilot, Joe Purshark. I was first out, so I picked him up to take him to the hotel. Before concluding the three-mile drive, the car stopped. The passenger asked if it would be all right for him to look under the hood. We fumbled around in there until we got the car started. I took him around for the rest of his stay so he saw how much trouble I had with that car. When he was leaving, he told me he had a 1969 Fleetwood Cadillac that he would put on the boat for me and he would come back in two weeks. He even paid the freight and duties. When the car arrived in Providenciales, I didn't have any money to pay him for it. He didn't mind, saying he would set it up with his old friend, Mr. Russ De'Coudres, that I make payments to him for the car.

Things began to get better at that point. I didn't have so much trouble with that car. I taxied for a while, still looking for another job right along, but didn't find one. In September 1980, we had another beautiful daughter, Lacal. Our family was growing steadily. In 1979, after being home for three years, my wife got a job at the Five Cays Primary School, now the Enid Capron Primary School.

In 1980, we started Palmer's Tire, a small shop in the yard, and I wanted my wife to stay in the shop so I could continue to taxi. She didn't agree. She liked teaching. But she couldn't drive, so I had to take her to school in the morning and pick her up in the afternoon. I was closing the shop too much. Sometimes when I got back from dropping her off, I would meet a note saying, "Charlie, I was here for two tires or a battery, but no one was here. If I don't find it over the road, I'll be back this afternoon." By the time I go to pick them up and come back, I would meet another note saying, "I was here for the second time, and no one was here." I couldn't taxi often because business wasn't good enough to hire someone to run the shop. I was burning forty dollars a week in gasoline, and Zen was making about thirty dollars a week teaching, but still she wasn't ready to stop. The shop wasn't doing too well. For me, it was some days driving taxi and some days staying in the shop.

Someone else opened a tire and auto parts shop shortly afterward. Even though our prices were better, it didn't make a difference. People preferred to go three miles to purchase what they needed at a higher price. I decided to fix tires for less and mount them free as an incentive to the customers, but that didn't work either. The only time I would see customers was when all the other shops were closed or after I went to bed. Then they wanted me to get out of bed to fix their flats. During opening hours, they would pass straight by. The only other time I would see some of the local people was when they wanted credit. If I gave them credit, they talked about me. If I didn't, they talked also. I often wonder what I did to my people, especially the people of Blue Hills. Business got so bad at one stage that Mr. Bill Dudson told me I could fix his building he had on Leeward Highway and use it for a small fee while he wasn't using it. I moved there with the tires and auto parts in one side and a snack bar on the other.

During this time, we had a fourth daughter, Sabrina. So I called the snack bar "Sabrina's Snack Bar." Johnston International was building the new airport, so things were booming. But my wife is a Christian, so she didn't help in the selling of the beer and wine. I asked her again to leave school and run the business, but she still didn't want to even before I moved the tire business on Leeward Highway. I asked one of the bosses at Johnston for a job as a truck driver. He told me they were expecting another truck on the island, and as soon as it arrived, they would hire me. I found out later that some of the locals told them I was too troublesome.

We didn't have city water yet, so when we built houses, we built cisterns large enough to separate the spring water from the rainwater and desalinated water. This water had to be trucked in. I bought a water truck. Zen still didn't leave school. Spring water was being sold for fifty dollars per two thousand gallons and desalinated water for one hundred and twenty dollars. I still had a problem. The times people called for water, I had to close the shop to make deliveries. When shop customers were looking for me, I was in the water truck. Then Napa Auto Parts moved just up the street from me and almost put me out of business. The water business was good, however, so I moved back home to the first shop and ran the truck.

When I first got into the water business, there were only two others: Provident Ltd. and Provo Transportation. The name of my company was Custom Water Delivery Services. I had prompt, reliable service, and people got to like my business because they could depend on me. Big companies like Johnston International and Leeward Marina allowed me to haul their water so I was usually busy. People were telling others that I only was delivering eighteen hundred gallons, and their trucks were two thousand gallons, but that didn't bother me. We all had the same-sized tank; that was just a way to keep me down.

I would start at six in the morning and work until midnight sometimes. I always got the job done even if I had to stay up all night repairing a pump. The first type of pumps I used broke down so often that I had to change them and look for a different brand. At one point, I even tried selling used cars and trucks, but most people came to me when they were desperate. For that reason, I still have money out on the streets from each aspect or section of business I tried.

During those years, I built a new piece on my house. One of my supervisors from the 1970s, Michael Tucker, built it for me. He promised he would do a good job building, but he did a fantastic job. I was so pleased that I had him build two other houses in Blue Mountain on my wife's property. I originally had wanted to build an apartment building but wasn't allowed to do so. The building inspector came and looked at the property at my request and confirmed that I could build an apartment complex. So I went ahead and got the plans drawn, only to be told after all my efforts that I couldn't put an apartment building there. I was greatly disappointed because the inspector had already given me permission to build my wall of native stones and dig the hole for the cistern and septic tank. Then I got called into the office and was told that the area wasn't zoned for apartments. I had to go back to the architect and pay additional money to get plans for two houses.

My government destroyed my dreams but allowed an expat to come in to the same area and build his apartment complex. I remember Michael Tucker each time I look at these beautiful houses. He died in 1997 after a short illness. I should not have been surprised at my government. I had long tried to get a piece of property in the town area to move my business to but never was able to get a positive reply. Each time I asked different officials, it was a different story until there wasn't anything left they would say. Yet, years later, people are still coming from other islands and countries and obtaining property in that area. Even as I write this book, new owners are moving into that area.

I got the same negative response each time I approached my government about anything. I preferred for my children to get higher education in the United States because they would be exposed to more technology and life was a little easier. I knew my government didn't give scholarships to the United States, but some investors and well-wishers donated scholarships that people from Providenciales didn't benefit from. Students from the other islands, especially Grand Turk (the capital city), were usually the beneficiaries. Most of the time though, these contributors were investing in Providenciales or residing here.

Everything has its season, and this was the water season. A man wanted to join me as my partner in the water business. I told him I didn't need any partners, so he influenced another native to get licensed as a proprietor, so he could get his own trucks. Well, as soon as he had the license in his hand, he bought the native man's share and got him out of the business. Many of our people got licenses for persons who couldn't get them for themselves and got put out of the company as soon as the license was produced. With so many water truck owners now, business began to decrease for the small man, and this new guy had most of the business. Local truckers began to complain of the lack of business while the expat was flourishing.

One day, they invited me to a meeting to discuss the situation of the native and his deceptive deal with this expat. It was decided that we would look into the idea of revoking the deceptive license as soon as possible. One of the truckers attending that meeting contacted the expat and let him know what we had decided. He became partners with that same man later on. They were the only ones making real money after that. The rest of us were merely paying bills. I tried with my trucks for as long as I could and got rid of them in 1998.

Early in 1993, my brother and I decided to start a restaurant, Pub on the Bay, in Blue Hills. As soon as we started fixing up the building we were about to use, the people in the immediate area became uneasy. In just a few days, the people's representative came across with a petition signed by most of the neighbors, stating they didn't want a nightclub there. They didn't even stop to find out what we were doing before they tried to get us out. I think that was the only time I saw the representative in that place of business, and I was involved there for seven years.

Government officials and heads of departments gave me a hard time on many occasions. During the building of the huts on the beach, I had approval to begin building, but still an officer came to stop the work because people around wanted to stop my progress. At other times, I came under direct attack, opposition, or discrimination from government officials who I thought should protect me. I wanted to put up a signpost on Blue Hills corner to advertise the restaurant in Blue Hills. I went to planning and got approval before doing anything.

As soon as I put a carpenter there to erect the sign, officials from the same office came and stopped him again. I had to go back to the office and find out why. They allowed it to be put up, but I couldn't keep it there for long. They soon found a reason why I had to remove it. A law came into effect that said I would be charged twenty thousand dollars or serve jail time if I didn't remove it within a certain time. So it had to go, but other signs that were there along with mine are still there after all these years with no problem. I suppose my wrong was to be affiliated with the wrong party and make that known.

In my quest for a livelihood, many changes took place, some positive and some negative. My brother left our partnership after an incident between his girlfriend who worked with us and me. He went on his own and opened a seafood restaurant in a different location. Chefs we had also left at different times so I was left with two helpers who ended up being cooks. They learned while watching the others and became just as good or better. They made me very happy when I discovered they could do the job. Customers always commented on how well the food was prepared and the delicious taste. We were busy because of the European-plan hotels on the island. Tourists could come out and visit other restaurants. They frequented Pub on the Bay, and it became one of their favorites.

There was one problem, however, because the hotels were in the Bight and Grace Bay. The taxi fare to Blue Hills was high, so I purchased a van to help transport them in. We heard from tourists that the taxi drivers didn't talk about or promote Pub on the Bay even if they could afford to come. The hotel employees did tell them about Pub on the Bay when they said they were interested in eating native foods and learning how we lived. Whenever they ate at Pub on the Bay, they would comment that it was the best food they had on the trip.

In February 1997, the Pub on the Bay made it into the *International Gourmet* magazine! It is the only local restaurant so far in Turks and Caicos to enjoy such an honor. Some of the restaurant owners were asking me how much money I paid to get into such a prestigious magazine. I didn't buy that article though. It was just natural. Since then, the *International Gourmet* magazine has written to find out if I would share my recipes for publication, especially my conch chowder. I have not written back to them yet. I think I would like to talk to a representative and find out exactly what they would want before I decided.

The changes continued as the government allowed all-inclusive hotels to operate in the islands. The tourists in these hotels stayed in because everything was provided for them on-site as a package deal. The general support from the tourists for our restaurant decreased since they weren't free to come and go as they wished. Inevitably, my business decreased and that of other locals as well. These all-inclusive hotels brought in a high percentage of their workers so our people ended up getting the lower-paid positions or nothing at all. I think, when the tourists come, they want to travel around the island and see what we have to offer and meet some of us. The all-inclusive idea is for countries where the crime rate is extremely high and people are afraid to go out. We need our tourists coming out and mingling with the local people, and our local people should be able to get jobs. It would be a smart thing for our government to make sure our people are being provided for by making sure the people receive the education they need for survival. We want our people growing along with our country and not lagging behind because they lack education.

I will always respect Sir Lynden Pindling, former prime minister of the Bahamas, because he made sure Bahamians were qualified to fill various positions in their country. This is what we should do as part of the development process. The people of Turks and Caicos are friendly and hospitable. We try to be nice to all our visitors and do not intend to change that. At the same time, we want what's ours in peace and harmony. We want to grow with the country and enjoy promotion and prosperity along with everyone else. So I hope our government will soon realize that we need a chance to be fully educated and take our proper place. Our people, on the other hand, should strive to be the best we can be, all of us. Our government also needs to look into raising the minimum wage so people with low-paying jobs can still be able to survive while trying to educate themselves and maintain a livable standard of living. I care very much about the future of the people and want to show them that I care and help them to do right. I learned that from my parents during my developing years and want to pass it on to future generations.

Growing up with Ma Tiny was rough, but there were also good times. She taught me to know and do right. I grew up in church, learning to love the Lord, respect the elderly, help the weak, love my neighbor, and own up to a fault if I was wrong. So I do not know how to hold grudges, even with all the difficulties I have had. I once asked Ma Tiny if I could invite Zen home for dinner after church. In those days, white rice and corned beef mixed with spaghetti in tomato sauce was top dish. Anyway, she cooked the rice before we left for church and hurried home ahead of us to prepare the corned beef and spaghetti. As we got to the house, she asked me to open the corned beef can for her. I told her to give me a chance to remove my jacket before I did it for her.

She must not have heard me because, as I turned my back, I felt something hit me behind my neck. I felt a burning sensation and warm liquid streaking down my clothes. Before I knew it, she had hit me with that can, and I was bleeding. My white shirt quickly became red with my blood. She thought I was being disrespectful and decided not to allow that to happen. She was already mad because she messed up trying to open the corned beef. At that point, I was so embarrassed that I told Zen to go home while I nursed my wound. I didn't get mad and curse or do anything rude. I believe, "He who curseth father or mother will die the death." I know this because Mr. Seymour was the perfect example. I have the scar from that wound and will take it to my grave. It still could be seen on my neck to this day.

Like I said earlier, there were good days and good times, like going to church as a family. Ma Tiny was the Sunday School superintendent, and Baba became a deacon later on. So I was in church service six times each Sunday. At six o'clock, we went to prayer meeting. At nine o'clock, we had to be in Sunday school. We moved right into the worship service at eleven o'clock. And before we knew it, we were heading back to afternoon Sunday school at three o'clock. Some Sundays, we had inquirers class before going home. At seven thirty, we attended evening service. They taught me to sing, love the Lord, and pray. You could see why I held no resentment against them. They taught me well. I think they helped me to raise my children to be the best any parent would want their children to be. I am very, very grateful to them now for their timely and fair upbringing.

My mother was a kindhearted person who always entertained strangers and was always prepared to share whatever she had, no matter how small her portion was. She didn't have to know you to make a gift for you and welcome you into her home. She would give whatever she thought you needed, perhaps money for this one, foodstuff for the next, and clothes for the other. She never stopped giving. I know God blessed her time and time again. She suffered from diabetes later on in life and until the time of her passing. She was also nearly deaf, and many times, I felt sorry for her and cried for her.

My father was also a good and honest man from the time I knew him. As a boy, I would hear him say how his father had left a parcel of land for him and his sister Jane had to get forty acres. I would have liked it if he had left a will before he died, but he didn't. These land stories often make families fall apart, and I don't want that kind of thing. I was given to my father and stepmother at the age of nine months for them to nurture and bring up. My father told me I was Ma Tiny's own child since she didn't have any more children. They brought up many other children, mostly my father's children or relatives' children, but I always knew I was special. Yet I always felt that, if Mommy had kept me, I would have been able to obtain a better education because she made sure the rest of her children stayed in school.

I am the eldest of her children, but as far as I can remember, we never really got along. I often wonder if it's because I didn't get a good education or because we didn't grow up in the same household. They always kept their distance and assumed Mommy loved me better than she loved them. They would even suggest that to her. I realize she loved all of her children equally, so I practiced listening to what she had to say before talking back. I try to maintain a love for them though, whether they like it or not. After all, we have the same blood.

Baba and Ma Tiny brought up his daughter Francis's last son because Francis died while he was a young baby. They were the only parents he knew. We lived together as a family, and I was like his big brother. Later, another boy child, the son of one of Ma Tiny's nieces, came to live with us as a baby. I taught these boys many things as a big brother. Sometimes it's amazing to watch situations develop and change before one's eyes. During my growing years, I was made to do all the work, but another fellow younger than me was allowed to get out where he wished as long as he liked. He had no responsibilities. Soon he began to steal from whomever, and then he started to steal from my father and then me. My house and shop were located in the same yard as my father's. The house is about fifty feet away, and the shop is sort of in the middle of both houses. Because of the closeness, it was easy to know when we were home and when we were out.

We were operating Palmer's Tire then and had established a certain place to keep money that only my wife and I knew about. At time, I would put away a few hundred dollars, knowing only my wife besides me knew where it was. Later when either of us checked it, it would be a few hundred dollars less. I couldn't understand it and began to wonder if my wife was putting money aside for herself. The bank came to Providenciales from Grand Turk once per week back then, so money had to be secured until the next week. As far as I was concerned, I thought our money was safe until I started missing some. I knew I wasn't senile but could never figure out what was going on. It never occurred to me that my little adopted brother would steal from me.

I got almost to the point of blaming my wife but never said anything to her. Every day, I was missing money and would mention it. Well, I was a bit on the wild side, so my wife probably thought I was only saying that to find a story to tell her and giving the money to some girl. I, on the other hand, felt she didn't love me and was saving money to leave.

I consoled myself by thinking, "If she wants to steal from herself, that's fine with me. As far as I'm concerned, I'm trying to build a future for my family and me."

This mystery continued in my house as well as in my father's until one day Baba confronted me with his theory of what was happening. He told me how he was constantly missing money and wanted to find out if I was the one doing that to him. I was very hurt and wondered how he could think I would do something like that to him. I thought about how I had lived with him all those years and they have never missed any money. Now I was in my own house and going back there to steal money. I would have never thought about that even though they worked me from the age of thirteen without giving me anything substantial.

My father kept on missing money so he decided to set a trap for me and waited around for me to take the bait, but he lost. Later on, he told me how he decided to prove I was stealing from him. He put some money in a special place, pretending he was going out. I was going to take Zen to school so that, when I got back, I would go in the house before he got there. After I left, he went back home, hid himself, and waited for me to come back and try to enter his property unknown to him or anyone else. He was disappointed, yet relieved, when I returned home and went into my house and stayed there. He was hiding in a little house they used to keep pots and pans, expecting to see me sneaking across the yard to enter his house to steal. He knew that I knew Ma Tiny was at the airport selling lunch because I had taken her there. So he couldn't figure out what was the holdup. After a long time, he came out of hiding and checked the money, and it was gone. He knew it couldn't have been me because he was watching me. He met the boy in the house, and then it clicked. He began to question him about the money and told him he would call the police if he didn't tell him the truth. He then gave him the money and admitted to taking the rest.

When my father told me this story, I cried at seeing how my own father was looking at me in a negative way. This episode didn't make a difference in this boy's life though. He continued to take money from me every chance he got. One day as soon as we left to take Zen and the children to school, he took that chance and went into my house. One of the neighbors saw him that time and told me about it as soon as I returned. He even showed me how he saw him going in through the window. His footprints were still fresh. He even made footmarks on the children's bed he jumped on. I was angry with him, so angry, that I told him to stay away from me as far as possible.

Things began to get worse though, and my parents didn't know what to do. In 1977, my father came to me with the documents for the property he had in North West Central, a parcel of one hundred and sixty acres that we still own. He told me he wanted me to keep it safe for him so that, if anything happened to him, I would have it. The next year, he came back, asked for it so he could check on something, and never brought it back. I wondered what was happening but never asked about it again. Two years later, he came back to find out if I had the document. I reminded him that he had taken it back about two years earlier. I could see he didn't believe me, but I knew it was the truth. He had this questionable look on his face as he left.

"Well, who has it then?"

About a month later, an expat called me by telephone and said: "I think I have something you would be interested in. You can come to my house to see it and bring one hundred dollars." I couldn't figure out what he had until I got to his house that evening. I was very surprised when he produced my father's land paper. "How did you get this? My father was looking for this everywhere." He informed me, "Your stepbrother sold it to me for one hundred dollars. But, since I know you and your father, I can't keep it." I did not take it from him, but I told him I would let my father come for it himself. I heard through the grapevine later that this man had contacted his attorney in connection with obtaining title to my father's property but found out he couldn't do anything with that. My father had already reported it lost to the land registry. Baba paid him the hundred dollars and got the paper from him.

Again, I thought, *How could my father believe I would try to take from him what is his?*

But he found out who was trying to destroy him in the end.

While we are on the subject of land, my great-grandmother had three sons with my great-grandfather before he died and then she had another son after his death. These men worked as fishermen, and then two of them went to the United States in search of a better life. My grandfather stayed at home with his father, who later died. Before he died, he told my grandfather that since he stayed to be near him, the property would come to him and his son after him. My grandfather died after being sick for a while, while my father was still young and unable to administer or represent himself to secure what was his. Since no will was drawn up, my great-grandmother gave some of the same property to her last son. I guess his grandmother thought he didn't know he was supposed to be the heir. By the time my father started to contact his uncles in the States, it was too late. He only got the small portion his father's house was built on, with his house on the same plot. When my grand-uncle came home from the Bahamas to check on the property, he told my father we would have to build a wall around ours. He put down boundaries and showed us where they were so we could build our wall.

Shortly after that, he died and left everything to his daughter, who came later to see where the property was. She was quite friendly with my father and me while he was alive. I still feel it is a good thing for people to make wills so their property can be distributed the way they would like it to be after they are gone. I spoke to my father several times about preparing a will, but he never did. He always said that if he died before his wife, she would stay in the house until her death. And then it would belong to Lenny, his grandson. I knew that was his wish and so did my brother and sisters, and we had no problem with that.

My brother Mackie's house is also on the same property that my father's house was on. My lot was cut off a long time ago after I built the shop. The shop was built partly on my father's portion, but he said that was no problem to him because that was only a few feet over. His instruction to me wasn't to allow the lot to be divided because brothers should be able to live as one. But that didn't or couldn't work. It was easier said than done. I wished he had made a will or divided the property how he wanted it to be. That would have made life so easy. Each person would know exactly what belonged to him or her. Eventually, I built a wall to separate my and Mackie's properties.

During the period when my father was administrating on the property at North West Central that his father had left, some people told the court that he was a liar and didn't have that amount of land he was saying he had. Baba had gotten that property documents straight after losing it in the 1945 hurricane but lost it again during the 1960 hurricane. Mr. Clement Howell, the then-headmaster of the primary school, and Stanley Williams, the corporal custom and immigration officer for Providenciales, testified on his behalf in regards to his credibility. Persons in the audience knew the property belonged to him, so they added their testimony on his behalf as well. Yet he ended up making the same mistake his father and grandfather made by leaving no will.

He used to tell me that since they brought me up from a baby and since his wife didn't have any more children, I was their special child. "The rest of the children stayed for a while and then left, but you stuck by us, therefore you will get what's mine. And Tiny says the same thing."

They said this many times over, especially about the property in North West Central. Of course, I couldn't just go by that because that was only cheap talk. Nothing was in writing.

They did have some serious talk between them though because, as soon as I got home after my father's death, my stepmother gave me all of the property documents.

I questioned her, "What am I supposed to do with this?" She replied "He only told me to give it to you." She said, "I know you will look after me until I die. I don't want any of the land. You can have her share because you are just like my son." As I sit here in the living room of my house, I look directly at the spot where my father's house was. It had to be demolished a few years after my stepmother's death because no one was living in it and it was decayed. It hurts my heart to look over there and reminisce how much I had to clean the yard so often as I grew. I smile when I remember how I used to think that was the best house in Providenciales.

⚜

Sometimes I used to hear people say who their role models were, and I wondered why they chose persons who were distant. I feel like parents ought to live in a way that their children will want to follow them. That is what I did. I watched my father and set out to be like him. He was careful with what he said, respected everyone, dressed well, and worked hard. His conversations were educational, and he was well respected in this country. I want to do the same for my children. I always tell them to be the best they can be and make a worthwhile contribution not only in Turks and Caicos, but also in the world.

My father was a Baptist preacher for many years, and I have never heard anyone speak badly of him. He was well-liked, kind, and understanding and helped everyone he could. We were close friends, especially in my later years. We used to chat for hours when we had time. After he sold the *Wheeland Queen*, he had to use his dinghy to fish in. He had a six-horsepower Johnson engine that made him slower compared to his colleagues who had bigger engines and faster boats. They would always leave him behind because his boat was so slow. Trips to West Caicos took forever it seemed.

I bought him a fifteen-footer skiff with a used seventy-horsepower Mercury engine. Ivy Hall, one of his nieces, wanted to help him out as well, so she bought him a brand-new forty-horsepower Johnson engine. This engine leg was short so he took the boat to Walkin Marine and cut the stem down. Sherlock Walkin did a good job on the boat. We bought it back to Blue Hills and put it in the water, and you would never guess what he did. He asked Cyril to go with him and left me standing there on the beach. I was surprised, me having the boating experience, standing on the beach without a glance from my father.

They got out on the water and fought and fought. They came in for lunch and went back. He was supposed to check the engine out

154

and make sure everything was okay and ready for the season. This was the day before the Caicos Bank reopened for lobster season.

By this time, I had decided to relax at home, thinking by now they had everything figured out. We had only two channels for television back then so whatever came on was good. I had just begun to watch a western movie with Alan Ladd, one of my favorite actors. I heard a knock on the door. It was Baba. I went to see what he wanted. He had made all his preparations and got everything placed into the boat, and he was ready to go to Five Cays to begin fishing the next morning early. He came now for me to take the boat to Five Cays for him. By this time, all his fishing buddies had gone. He was the last one behind. What amazed me, though, was that he didn't ask me if I could do it. He told me what he wanted. I was enjoying this movie with my wife and felt hurt because I had been home all day and could have been finished with that task if I had started earlier. By now, the sun was almost set. I got angry but didn't let him know it. I changed into my swim trunks, T-shirt, and slippers. I joined Baba, Cyril, and Lenny waiting at the beach for me.

As I jumped in the boat, I noticed they didn't have the six-horsepower engine with them. I told them we needed it in case the new engine had a problem. Well, I was glad I did. As soon as we got outside of Wheeland Cut, out on the ocean, the big engine made a different sound, but I paid no attention to it. Of course, I was at the wheel. (They told me to take it as soon as I got in the boat.) Some big rollers were coming inside, so I told them to brace themselves. As we tried to get around North West Point and on to Sam Bay, the engine quit. I had to think fast because our anchor couldn't touch the bottom of the ocean.

Quickly, I placed the six-horsepower engine on the stern and started it up. I coaxed her around the point while trying to get as close as possible to the shore to avoid the big waves that billowed around us while trying to turn the boat wherever they wished. When I got close enough to the shore, I looked at the forty-horsepower engine. As I raised the top of the engine, I noticed a loose wire. Upon closer inspection, I found the throttle loose. Having no tools to work with, I hitched it up somehow.

By then, the sun had almost set, and I had but a glare of light to work with. We managed to reach Five Cays by seven o'clock that evening. I told Baba to make sure he let Sherlock check the engine before he went out fishing the next day. As I left them on Five Cays beach, I wondered why I wasn't asked to help with the engine earlier to make sure it was working properly. If he had asked me then, we would have known before that something needed to be fixed. He would have been able to save the first day of the season to make a good catch like everyone else. Lobster season begins on August 1 each year, and everyone likes to be out on the water early to see how much lobster can be caught for that day. I still think he was all right though!

Now the old dinghy was sitting on the beach falling apart. Small boat regatta was a very popular activity then and held often. One day, I looked at that boat and decided to fix it up for racing. I asked Mr. James Dean to do some repairs on it for me. He laughed when I told him about my idea to put this baby in the next race. He said this boat wasn't built for racing, but to be a conch boat. At my request, he did the necessary repairs, and I bought all the items I needed to convert it into a boat to race. At its completion, it looked like a brand-new boat. We had no kind of idea how it would sail. Mr. Dean had a good laugh as we planned. Little did he know how that boat would sail. At that time, he was the racing champion. With all the repairs done and outfitted with new mast boom, sail, strouds, and a fresh coat of paint, we put it in the water. I had not, as yet, thought of a name for it. Ma Tiny came to the beach to watch as we took the boat out.

She watched for a few seconds. "Give that boat name the SS *Stinger Poop*."

We had a good laugh that afternoon, but that was the name, and that was exactly what the boat did. The name was written on, and the boat was ready to go with two fifty-pound bags of sand for ballast until I could find the right ballast.

The Dean families were very good boat builders and captains. George, James's nephew, wanted to be captain for the race. So he took it out for the trial run. He wanted me to go with him, but I wanted to stay on shore to watch with my father and Mr. Dean. Before the jib was hoisted, we realized that the boat going to sail fast. Mr. Dean looked at me and cleared his throat. He knew he had competition. He had to admit that boat was fast. Everyone watching it from the beach became excited just thinking what was going to happen in the race, which was about a week away. When George returned to the beach, he was speechless with excitement and surprise at the boat's performance. He didn't know what to say. He realized a heavy blow had been dealt to the champion. We left the riggings on because the race was so close. We could hardly wait because expectation was so high now.

My brother-in-law Henry Williams, also a good boat captain, told a story of how he was thinking to come and have a mini race with the SS *Stinger Poop* one afternoon when he was bringing his boat from Thompson Cove Marina. His boat, the SS *Indigo*, was much bigger and could sail very well. George and I were out practicing and having a little fun with the SS *Stinger Poop*. He said from his observation of the SS *Stinger Poop* that his mind was quickly changed because he thought the boat did look too crazy out there and moving too fast through the water. He didn't want to look bad. We wanted Mr. James to bring out his boat for a practice run, but he refused.

On the morning of the regatta, I woke up early to run an errand before the race started. I looked at the SS *Stinger Poop* calmly rocking in the gentle breeze and was confident she could win first prize in her class. I had her anchored in the harbor just in front of my dwelling home, so I could always keep an eye on her. I was excited after a good night's rest. On my way back home, when I thought I should be able to see the boat, I didn't. As I got closer, however, I saw the mast in shore. I parked the truck and went to see what had happened.

My captain was changing the riggings. He told me he was trying to do something different because he thought she wasn't rigged correctly to win. I wondered about that but didn't say much because it was too late to find a new captain. All the good captains were already connected to an owner and a boat. Since I almost got drowned as a child, I didn't want to sail myself. But to me, the whole trip was mysterious, the trim of the boat, the way we sailed, and how the boat almost sank more than once. It was finally figured out when we got to the buoy in front of the Island Princess Hotel. To avoid the SS *Stinger Poop* from coming in first, the boat was gently swerved so the other boat could come in first. Despite all the efforts to delay the SS *Stinger Poop*, she still came in second. All the onlookers saw and were amazed. He didn't want his uncle to feel bad, but I settled for second place.

I now regret not passing that trophy onto my father for his enjoyment and remembrance of his little conch boat.

Chapter Four

Life, Death, and the Tides of Change (1980s)

After completing the building for the shop in the yard, I used to tell him to watch the yard for me anytime I was going away for supplies or a trip. He always appreciated that and felt useful and wanted.

On November 3, 1989, I was leaving for one of those shopping trips when the flight came earlier than I expected. I called a taxi driver to pick me up to avoid leaving my truck at the airport since I was going for a few days. Gus Lightbourne, the taxi driver, called me from the airport. He told me the plane was on the ground, and he was on his way for me. I had to hurry shower and dress before he reached the house. When I went to get into the taxi, my father was out in the yard beside a load of quarry, showing a workman how he wanted it to spread out. I looked over there to tell him I was leaving, but he wasn't paying attention. I felt like waving at him, but he still wasn't looking my way. I had to leave to catch the flight.

When I got to the airport, the passengers were boarding so I had to hurry, but my mind stayed on him. Even during the flight, I kept thinking about him. I arrived in Miami, checked into the Marina Park hotel, and called my driver to pick me up so I could do some shopping until nine o'clock. We stopped to eat and got back to the hotel at eleven. I often took advantage of the water when I went away so I took a nice, long shower and went to bed. That night, I had a dream that my best friend Bob Jones was in an accident. I had met this guy in the 1970s when I was managing the Erebus Inn. We became close because he owned a small hotel also, the Park View.

159

His hotel was in Miami, and I stayed there many times after getting to know him.

He helped me out a great deal by purchasing supplies and shipping them to me. He purchased my first water truck and shipped it to Providenciales. I would send him the money, or he would advise me to keep it until he came back to Providenciales. In the dream, his girlfriend Marsha was with him in the car. She had many cuts and bruises but was alive. He, on the other hand, didn't have any visible damage but was dead. When I awoke, I couldn't sleep anymore that night but waited anxiously for morning so I could call Bob to see if he was all right.

The next day, I went shopping as usual and came back late again. As I returned for the night, I told my driver I was going to be rich some day because I was going to win the Florida lottery. From that time, I played every opportunity I could get. I told him my dream from the night before and then went up to my room. As I finished my shower, the phone rang. I picked it up and wondered why someone would call so late. Then I assumed it must be my driver, wanting to find out what time I wanted to be picked up the next day. But no, it was Zen.

She was struggling to tell me something I didn't want to hear. "Your father is dead."

"How did it happen?"

She was trying to tell me a story that I didn't really understand until later. He went to fetch a bucket of water for Ma Tiny from the catchment. When he was finished, he laid down across the bed. Ma Tiny noticed something different about the way he was lying down, so she called him, and he didn't answer. She went over and shook him, but he didn't move. Then she called the other people in the house, and they checked him out. He was dead. They called Dr. Menzies, who upon his examination, pronounced my father dead.

I sat in my hotel room and thought. I hadn't gotten to say good-bye. He was gone from this life forever. I didn't sleep at all that night. Early the next morning, I called my driver to take me to the airport to go home. I went to stay until Tuesday, but I had to leave on Saturday. I mustered enough courage to buy a black suit for myself and then headed for the airport, hoping I would get on the flight since I didn't have a reservation. I did get on the flight and reached home still dazed, not sure I could accept the fact of my father's death. His body had already gone to Grand Turk for autopsy. My wife told me that after Dr. Menzies pronounced him dead, he took his body up to his clinic, where he left the AC running all night to keep him cool until the next morning when they would take him to Grand Turk to the morgue.

I busied myself with building the tomb and preparing for the funeral. The same cousin who had bought the engine for him called and said she would like to buy the casket, so she shipped it to Grand Turk where his body was prepared for burial. The following Saturday, my brother and nephews went with me to the airport to pick up the body, which Ma Tiny's nephew Rudith Outten had shipped from Grand Turk. We placed his body in the Bethany Baptist Church where the funeral service was to be held the next day.

This church is only a few seconds walk from where we live. We had a wake that night, and many people attended and spoke well of my father and how he lived. The funeral the next day was well attended too. I never got over his death though. I always wished he had lived to see Wayne graduate from university. Wayne was the first one in our family to graduate from university. He always used to say Wayne would make it to the top, but he didn't live to see it happen. He would joke about him being smart because he got that from him. He would have been very proud of Wayne's accomplishments.

After he died, the boat I bought for him went to Ma Tiny. There were two men, Haitians Baba had gotten work permits for and who worked along with Baba, and they continued to work the boat. That helped to support her, along with whatever help me and others gave. They stayed around for quite a while.

Ma Tiny was a churchgoing person even though she treated me so mean during my growing years. Later in my life, she treated me fairly well. One thing I can say, she taught me the Holy Word. She believed in God, and she was a good singer. In my opinion, she was the best singer I ever knew. To me, she could sing prettier than Mahalia Jackson. I thought she had the voice of an angel. There were songs and hymns from the years gone by that most people had forgotten, but she would remember. People could always ask her, and she would be able to remember how the tune went or what the words were. I used to feel really proud to know she was my mother. I learned to sing because of her singing. She used to call me when she felt like singing, and we would sing songs until we were tired. Many times, I didn't know the words but would pick right up on the tune. She sang at different church concerts. Everyone enjoyed her singing. Sometimes she was called to sing more than once during any concert.

On May 10, 1992, I had a car come in on the boat, so I spent the whole day at the dock trying to get it cleared so I could bring it home. I left early Sunday morning, so I didn't go over to wish Ma Tiny a Happy Mother's Day, knowing I would do that in the afternoon upon my return. When I pulled up in the yard, after spending all day at the dock, I could see her sitting in her living room all dressed up and looking really good. She looked very happy. She greeted me before I had time to greet her. I didn't want it to happen that way because I wanted to get cleaned up, so I could hug her, kiss her cheek, and present her with a gift. But because she looked so expectant right then, I went into my house, got her gift, and went over to her house. I hugged and kissed her and gave her the gift I had for her. I stayed and talked for about fifteen minutes and then left. I was hungry and wanted to eat dinner. During our conversation, she told me that Lenny and his girlfriend had taken her out to lunch that day at the Banana Boat restaurant. Our conversation ended, so I left.

That evening, there was a concert at the Turquoise Reef Hotel, featuring the Cooling Waters, Ma Tiny's nephew's group. All of the men in the group were formerly from Turks and Caicos but living in the Bahamas. She had planned to attend, so she told Zen to let our older daughters go along with her. During the concert, she asked Vanessa to go to the bathroom with her. When she got into the cubicle, she began to groan. She was there for so long that Vanessa began to become afraid. She kept asking her if she were all right. Someone else came to use the bathroom and, after hearing her moans, told Pamela to go see what was happening. They were very attached to Ma Tiny and didn't want anything bad to happen to her. They called her Ma and my father Pa.

After they tried to get her out of the cubicle and saw they couldn't, they called for help. The doctor was immediately called and took her to the clinic. He kept her there for most of the night and then allowed her to come home. After they got her to the clinic, they called to let us know what was going on, so I went to the clinic to see her. She was in bed, but not quite lying down, kind of sitting with several pillows supporting her back and neck. I looked at her and held her hand. She opened one eye, looked at me, and closed it back. I started wondering right then if she would make it. I didn't know what her problem was, and I felt the doctor didn't know at that time exactly what was wrong, but he knew she was dying. I wondered about the lunch she had eaten earlier that day, but I could never figure it out. Several hours earlier, she was so happy. Now she was almost in a coma.

I was driving the same car I had picked up from the dock that afternoon. I went back inside of it, sat down, and thought for a while.

She hadn't complained during the week. She hadn't been feeling ill earlier.

So what's happening now? I thought.

As I sat there, I looked up to the Lord and told Him to let His will be done. I felt that was the last of Ma Tiny. While I was there thinking or praying, someone came to the car and told me the doctor said we could take her home.

Although I began preparing to take her home, I thought, *Why should I take her home in that condition?*

But I was convinced the doctor felt or knew she was dying and didn't want to tell us. She was so heavy when we tried to lift her to the car that it took six men to handle the weight. Her normal weight was two hundred pounds, which two men ought to be able to lift without a problem. I thought that was surely dead weight!

We got her home and in bed safely. She didn't say much but groaned every now and then. I watched her for a while, and then I told them I would go rest because I was very tired. I told them, though, to call me if they saw any difference in her. About five thirty Monday morning, someone came to call us. I told Zen to go, and I would take a shower before I went over. I already had the feeling that Ma Tiny was dead and knew I would have to take the body to the morgue in South Caicos. I felt that was the last of her. When Zen came back, she told me she was dead.

I calmly said, "I knew from the feeling I had inside."

I accepted that another long day lay ahead of me. I quickly got into some clothes and went round to the house.

I placed my hand on her forehead. "Good-bye, Mother. You were the best. I know you are in heaven now."

Then I went outside by myself and cried for a long time. As the news of her death spread, many people came to sympathize with us. After Doctor Menzies came and pronounced her dead, we placed her in a body bag in preparation for the trip to South Caicos. Doctor

Menzies wasn't the doctor who had attended to her the night before. I called Charles Air Services and chartered a plane to South Caicos. At the Thomas Brothers Morgue, before we left her, I zipped the bag open a little to look at her, and her eyes were opened. I closed them with my hands and zipped the bag again. Back in Providenciales, I started making funeral arrangements. I built her tomb just like my father's and right next to it. After it was completed, I went to Miami to get her casket and had it shipped to South Caicos. I didn't like the ones the Thomas Brothers had in stock and wanted to give her nothing but the best.

On that trip, I almost went to jail for the first time. I took some money with me to purchase items for the store but didn't have the courage to do so upon my arrival. I forgot to declare the amount of money on my customs form, and one of the officers asked me how much I was carrying. When I told her about fifteen thousand dollars, she took me to the security area. The officials there questioned me as to why I hadn't made a declaration, and I told them I forgot. They wanted to find out how I could forget something like that. I explained that my mother had just died, and they understood after I showed them the check I had written to Barclays Bank on my way to the airport. They expressed sympathy and allowed me to leave. After purchasing the casket and making sure it was delivered to the right address to be shipped on Turks Air, I purchased a suit for me and a nice dress for my wife. The things for the shop had to wait for another time. I headed back home. That's when trouble began.

Ma Tiny had one sister alive, but many nieces and nephews who came from the Bahamas and took over everything after all the hard work was done. Before they came, those of us who were here decided her funeral would be held at the Bethany Baptist Church where she worshipped and fellowshipped most of her life. I knew she would have liked to be buried there. But after this crowd came, most of those who were in agreement with the original plan changed on me and sided with the others to take the funeral service to the newest church building on the island, the Faith Tabernacle Church of God, an air-conditioned building with theatre-type seats, as opposed to the old building of Bethany Baptist with a few old fans and wooden benches. It had been around for many years and was very small, but I knew it would have been her choice since that was where she worshipped. I had already borrowed some tents to set up in the yard and many chairs, and I had planned to use TV monitors for those who were on the outside. The officers and members of Bethany were very helpful and agreed with me that it was the right thing to do. But her family wanted a big show.

So after I finished what I had to do, I was out of it. Everything they planned, they left me out. They didn't respect me being like her only child. They left me out. During the big funeral, I stayed home. It was a hard pill to swallow, knowing my stepmother, who I thought was my real mother for a long time until I realized differently, was going through the last exercise here on earth, but I couldn't be there with her. Not even to take my last look. It wasn't easy, but I fought it with tears in my eyes.

My family attended the funeral, and from what I heard, it probably was the biggest funeral ever in Turks and Caicos. People from all walks of life were there. She was a nice, well-known person whom everyone liked. She was known for her kindness, cooking, and singing.

To top all of this off, her sister called a meeting a few days after the funeral and invited me to it. When I arrived, I sat in the doorway. I didn't go inside because I was hurt and angry, and I thought a meeting should have been held before the funeral. Ma Tiny's sister took that opportunity to tell me that I had never loved her sister and didn't even respect her enough to attend her funeral.

I looked at that old woman in disgust but was glad I had learned to respect the aged, so I kept my mouth shut. I wanted to save my soul, so I controlled myself. If I didn't love Ma Tiny, she would have stayed in the Bahamas when they were trying to get her to do that after Baba's death. They told her, if she stayed in Turks and Caicos, I would take advantage of her, but she didn't listen to their foolish arguments. She told them she would come to Freeport for a few weeks and then come back to her children, Lenny, Cyril, Mackey, Jacynth, Lynn, my family, and myself. She wanted to spend her last years with us, and that she did. Her relatives in the Bahamas were shocked when she told them she missed us and was ready to return home. They told her all of her relatives were over there, but she insisted that, where her children were, was where she wanted to be. When this lady was finished telling me what she had to say, I told her thanks and left.

If I didn't love her, I could have left after I grew up or after I built two modern homes in Blue Mountain. I grew up in this yard, and my children did the same. I started living with her and my father when I was nine months old. My children are all grown. Most left to attend university and some are married and have their own children. I'm proud to say that those who are married got married right from our house.

I stayed with Ma Tiny all these years and looked after her as best I could. Even though I supposedly didn't love Ma Tiny, when her family left for the Bahamas, I had to take care of all of the bills. The savings account my stepmother and my father had together, her sister ended up with it because she was the nearest blood kin. And even after receiving this, she didn't even offer to help pay the bills. She kept all of the money for herself. I didn't mind though. Ma Tiny had been my mother, and I was glad I was able to pay her bills. I never went back to my father's house after that meeting.

A short while before she died, W.I.V. cable television produced a video with her speaking about the "good ole' days." She was taped sitting in front of her house with a beautiful oleander plant decorated with many flowers in the background. She mentioned my name several times during the interview and kept looking in the direction of my house to see if I was looking. She wanted me to be proud of her, and I was. She couldn't see me, but I was looking the whole time and was very proud of her. I am trying to acquire a copy of that tape so my grandchildren can know what she looked like. I am drawn close to her whenever they run that tape. She was a beauty, inside and outside. May her soul rest in peace!

Now that they are dead, I was left with all the problems. People I never heard about before their deaths came to tell me they should get a share of the property. I suppose they thought I didn't know any better so I would take their word for it and stress out myself. Even though Baba didn't leave any will, he told me many times who were involved in his estate. This situation in itself created enemies, but I only ignore people if I know I'm doing right. There is a saying that goes, "People will talk," so I live my life in accordance to what I know is right.

It would be impossible to please everybody in the world. I try to be friendly and helpful every chance I get. I lost about eighty-five thousand dollars (US) by selling tires or auto parts on credit, lending money to people who promised to pay back as soon as they got it. Delivering water with the hope of getting paid was tough. People leaving my rental property without paying didn't help. I never got anything easy. I worked hard most of my life. The only thing I got free was the documents to my father's property after his death.

Ma Tiny came to me with a maroon bag in her hand shortly after I got home, the next day after Baba's death. She said, "Your father said to give you this if anything happened to him. He said you would know what to do."

I looked inside, and it contained his property documents. I asked, "Are you sure I should get this?"

She said, "I'm sure."

"Did he say anything else?"

"No."

She had that confidence that I would take care of her. She told me so. So I decided, with the help of the Almighty God, I would take special care of her.

I take good care of my property as well because I worked hard to accomplish my goals in life. I didn't have the opportunity to acquire a good education. So one of my goals has always been to educate my children as best I could with the help of my wife and God. This made me very happy because some people wished my children wouldn't be able to make it. I am very thankful to God for health and strength to work and courage to see my children make it through. I am also very thankful for my faith in Him and belief in myself. My wife was with me all the way, and today we are proud parents of children who are happy to be the grandchildren of Baba and Ma Tiny.

I was unable to stay in school for long, but I put the little education I received to good use. I would like to mention some of my accomplishments at this point. I was the first person to own a new bicycle on the island, the first to fight against racism, the first who took the test and received my driver's license in Providenciales, and the second to own a four-kilowatt generator before we had city power. I was the first to build a modern house with shingle roof, the first native young man to manage a small hotel in the Turks and Caicos Islands, and the first islander to sell used cars. My restaurant, the Pub on the Bay, was the first to make it to the *International Gourmet* magazine from these islands, and still is the only one at this time. My son was the first valedictorian of the Provo High School, now Clement Howell High School, and I am very proud to be his father.

Sometimes, I can see the reason for the envy that people feel against me, but I thank God for His blessings because there are many more I can name. When I decided to send Wayne to university, people thought I didn't know what I was doing, so they concluded that I was crazy because they knew I couldn't afford to keep him there. I was determined to help him because he had graduated as top student in the Turks and Caicos Islands in 1990. Wayne moved to Henderson, Tennessee, in 1991 to attend Freed Hardeman University where he obtained a Bachelor of Science degree in biology with a minor in chemistry. Wayne later relocated to Memphis, where he resides to this day. Because of his quest for education, he didn't stop there. He went on and obtained a Bachelor of Science degree in psychology from the University of Memphis.

I had another highlight in my life recently. On May 7, 1999, I saw my son accomplish his dream. I knew then my labor hadn't been in vain. I saw my son receive his Master of Arts degree in political science with a concentration in public administration from the University of Memphis. I was a proud father and wanted everyone to know it. I sat in the front row reserved for Wayne's relatives. Other relatives also attended to celebrate the occasion as well. I appreciated them coming along to attend this great event in the life of our family. Wayne continued studying and received a Master of Arts degree in public administration from Columbia Southern University.

Wayne found the lady of his dreams, and they were married in 2001. They have three children. Wayne is currently the chief financial officer (CFO) at the St. Andrew Enterprise and president and chief executive officer (CEO) at Wealth Map Financial Network LLC. He had been asked to be the guest speaker at the tenth graduation exercise of the Clement Howell High School because he was the first valedictorian. It will always remain etched in my mind that Wayne was the first head boy, first valedictorian of the school, and guest speaker at my last child's graduation.

Pamela graduated as first salutatorian and later went on to the Turks and Caicos Community College (TCICC), where she obtained a diploma in business studies. It was my dream that she further her education, but she decided to start her career. She later met the man of her dreams, and they got married three years later in 1998. Pamela had a beautiful wedding, which many people attended. About five hundred guests and visitors enjoyed themselves. We fed them all, as well as others who showed up. There was much food and drink for everyone. Together, they have one daughter.

Pamela did several courses at the firm where she worked at that time as an accounts payable and payroll specialist. She returned to the TCICC a few years later and obtained her associate's degree in business administration. After twelve years of continuous employment at that firm, she was able to obtain a scholarship from them to attend Nova Southeastern University (NSU), where she obtained a Bachelor of Science degree in business administration.

After graduating from Clement Howell High School, Vanessa also attended the TCICC and obtained a diploma in hospitality studies. After the completion of her course, she attended Shelby State College in Memphis. Vanessa managed Pub on the Bay and Chaitalia Men's Store for the years they were in operation and continues to help with Blue Hills Bed & Linen. She has one son.

Lacal graduated as valedictorian from Clement Howell High School and then went on to the University of Memphis, where she obtained a Bachelor of Science degree in accounting. She worked for a few years at an accounting firm. Then she continued her studies at NSU and obtained her master's degree in accounting. She is currently head of finance at a major telecommunications firm. Sabrina, our baby, graduated as salutatorian, went on to NSU, and obtained her bachelor's degree in finance. She is currently employed at a trust company as a securities trader. She got married to the man of her dreams in 2009.

I have two other children who I am equally proud of, but I don't know the details of their lives because they don't live with me, but they are all my shining stars. Let me tell you, God has been good to me.

Let me tell you of God's continual goodness to me. I started playing the Florida lottery in 1988. I wasn't winning much, but I continued to play every chance I got. Sometimes I get the feeling I was spending or wasting too much money, but still I played. I never gave up hoping I would win one of these days. Even though I hoped, I never imagined it would happen. I usually played and then waited for Sunday to call Miami for the winning numbers.

At the restaurant, it was very slow. That week, as I sat outside hoping for someone to come for dinner or a few drinks, I prayed to God for help. He heard my prayer. That same night, Sherlock Walkin from Walkin Marina came there. We had a glass of wine, and then he told me he wanted to surprise his wife, Sandra, with a birthday party. He wanted to have it at Pub on the Bay. I think he brought me some good luck. They had a great time at the party.

On Sunday morning, September 19, 1999, I was a little tired from the party on Saturday night, but I wanted to attend church, so I got out of bed to go to the restaurant to clean up before church time. But my brown Ford truck that was always faithful to me would not start. I decided to look for a mechanic in Blue Hills but didn't find any. My cousin Jack Parker (Scrappy) lent me his truck to go to Five Cays to look for a mechanic. About two and a half miles out of Blue Hills, the truck ran out of gas.

What kind of hard luck am I experiencing? I thought.

By the time I got back home, it was after eleven. So I took a shower, sat on the bed, and began reading my Bible. I decided, since

I couldn't make it to church that day, I would study the Word for a while.

All of a sudden, I remembered that the Florida lottery was on during that time. So I called to get the numbers and found out there was only one winner. I hung up the phone and checked my numbers, which matched the ones I received over the telephone. My heart started beating rapidly, but I tried to contain myself. I had won! I thought I was dreaming, and to make sure I wasn't, I called another place for the numbers and received the same ones. I began to thank God for his goodness to me. I knew this wasn't just a stroke of luck. This was a blessing. I had two children in college in the United States and my family to take care of, and I was in bad shape economically. At the time I received the good news that I had won, I was home alone. My family was at church, and there was no one to tell. When they came home, I gave them the good news. They could hardly believe what they were hearing, but they were glad.

Epilogue

My advice to anyone would be, "Wait on the Lord." He knows our needs, and He rewards those who trust in Him. I am developing a hobby in golf, writing songs, and expecting a peaceful life.